# RETRO CROCHET

## Vibrant Vintage-Inspired Looks from the '70s, '80s, and '90s

### ASHLEE ELLE

Retro Crochet: Vibrant Vintage-Inspired Looks from the '70s, '80s, and '90s
Ashlee Elle

Editor: Kelly Reed
Project manager: Lisa Brazieal
Marketing coordinator: Katie Walker
Crochet tech editor: Tian Connaughton
Interior design: Jake Flaherty
Cover design: Jake Flaherty
Cover photographs: Ashlee Elle
Composition: Danielle Foster

ISBN: 978-1-68198-798-9
1st Edition (1st printing, June 2022)
© 2022 Ashlee Elle
All photographs © Ashlee Elle

Rocky Nook Inc.
1010 B Street, Suite 350
San Rafael, CA 94901
USA

www.rockynook.com

Distributed in the UK and Europe by Publishers Group UK
Distributed in the U.S. and all other territories by Ingram Publisher Services

Library of Congress Control Number: 2021944847

DEDICATED TO MY FAMILY, FRIENDS,
AND ALL THOSE WHO HAVE SUPPORTED THIS CRAFTY JOURNEY.
I APPRECIATE AND LOVE YOU ALL IMMENSELY!

# CONTENTS

# THE 1980s

# THE 1990s

# INTRODUCTION

I never imagined that my crafty beginnings would lead me here…

Crocheting started as a fun activity I did with my family. I'd gather around with my aunts on Fridays for craft night. We'd eat, talk, and laugh, and I learned the joys that came from a hook, yarn, and my own imagination. I fell in love with the endless possibilities and hoped that I'd get to a point where I could bring all the creations that dwelled in my mind to life. I've always loved art of all kinds: poetry, painting, photography, and there's just something so tangible about crocheting. An unmistakable connection between myself and the piece I'm making drew me in from the first stitch.

As I grew older and kept working at it, family and friends encouraged me to take my talents a step further. I started my crochet blog in 2010, cultivating a social media presence to share my work and found a community of other like-minded individuals who found beauty in bundles of yarn. The more I learned, crocheted, practiced, and experimented, the better I got and the more in love I became with the craft. I was bringing my dreams to life! It was only fitting that I called it The Dream Crochet.

The Dream Crochet has become my bastion of peace in a daunting world. It's easier for me to express my true feelings through art, and for that, I'm forever grateful. I've had my share of obstacles that I've had to overcome. At times, it can be difficult to make sense of it all. As an introvert, I'm not one to put myself out there for no reason, so crocheting became the outlet I needed to express what I keep hidden. The whimsical backgrounds, the stories, the handmade creations all helped me feel more myself! Passions can feel like such a frivolous thing, though when you create something with your heart, it puts everything into perspective. My true soul is never more apparent than when it's in the form of my art. My true self!

This craft has grown beyond my wildest imaginations, and now I get to present The Dream Crochet's *Retro Crochet* that will take you on a fashion journey through the '70s, '80s, and '90s with original and timeless pieces. This book will show how the past can be reimagined and brought into the modern era with wearable and stylish looks. It will be your guide to create handmade accessories and clothing influenced by generations of iconic staples we know and love with a fresh twist.

My greatest dream is that these designs will spark your own dream creations.

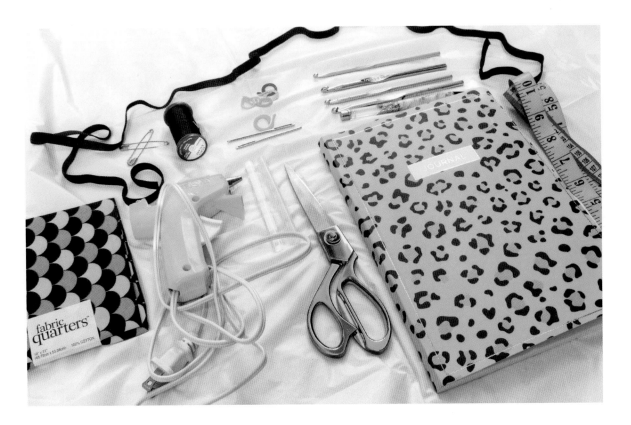

# MATERIALS & TOOLS

Before getting started on your crafty adventure throughout the crochet decades, making sure you have the right creative ingredients to accompany your crochet hooks and yarn through the projects will assist in making these handmade designs!

## SCISSORS

Always a crafty tool to have by your side, especially when it comes to cutting off strands of yarn!

## MEASURING TAPE

Measuring and focusing on gauge, along with personal measurements, truly helps with each crochet project. It also helps with guiding through a project with your customized details.

## CRAFT JOURNAL

A journal helps with keeping track of your projects. It's great for pops of inspiration, especially if you want to personalize a design by implementing unique and additional attributes.

## STITCH MARKERS

Markers assist in keeping your place when working in rounds to create crochet pieces, such as skirts and sleeves for your tops!

## SEWING NEEDLE & THREAD

Use for sewing the elastic bands together when creating the skirts and sewing notions directly to your crocheted pieces.

## YARN NEEDLE

Use to sew your crochet designs together and weave in ends (the leftover yarn tail) right into the stitches to conceal and clean the edges after and during the project.

## FABRIC FAT SQUARES

Implement lining for your crochet bags as well as accessories. Have fun selecting colorful prints to add a bit of personality to your handmade projects.

## ELASTIC BAND

Elastic bands create stretch at the waist when constructing waistbands for the skirts.

## APPLIQUES, CHARMS & ACCESSORIES

Add a bit of personalization throughout a design by selecting fun charms and accessories for your handmade creations.

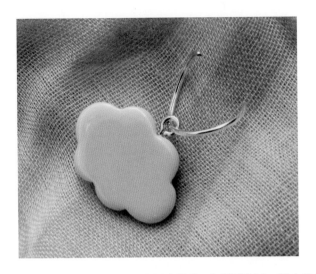

## METAL JUMP RINGS, METAL EARRINGS

Adjustable connectors are vital for assistance with constructing crochet jewelry and implementing notions to projects in personalizing a design!

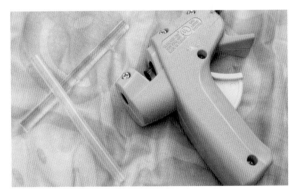

## METAL SUSPENDER CLIPS

To guide the crochet straps through the metal clip openings and attach them to your handmade crochet skirt.

## HOT GLUE GUN & HOT GLUE STICKS

A hot glue gun goes a long way when crafting! Assists in implementing appliques directly to your crochet projects, especially if sewing isn't your thing!

## ZIPPERS

Add a finished look to your crochet design, either by sewing or gluing the side of the zipper band onto your crochet accessory.

## NYLON WEBBING STRAPS [BUCKLE NON-ELASTIC STRAP]

To add and sew the notion of the back-pack straps to the very back of your crochet project.

# CRAFTY TIPS & TECHNIQUES

Throughout, the projects feature common and basic crochet techniques which will guide you in creating numerous designs and more!

## THE BASIC STITCHES UTILIZED THROUGHOUT

### Turning Chain

Turning chains assist in the height, as well as keeping your edges straight for your project. You will utilize the turning chain at the very beginning of each row.

- Single Crochet = 1TCH
- Half Double Crochet = 2TCHS
- Double Crochet = 3TCHS
- Treble Crochet = 4TCHS

# COMMON CROCHET TECHNIQUES USED

**STARTING CHAIN**

**SINGLE CROCHET**

**HALF DOUBLE CROCHET**

**DOUBLE CROCHET**

**TREBLE CROCHET**

## ABBREVIATIONS

- Chain(s) = CH(S)
- Double Crochet = DC
- Half Double Crochet = HDC
- Row = R
- RND= Round
- Single Crochet = SC
- Skip = SK

- Slip = SL
- Stitch(es) = ST(S)
- Turning chain(s) = TCH(S)
- Treble Crochet = TRC
- () work the instructions inside of the parentheses into the indicated stitch
- * repeat the instructions following an asterisk as many times as indicated

# ADDING THE DETAILS

## ADDING THE JEWELRY

Using the metal jump rings, you will separate them, guiding your crocheted projects, charms, or metal earrings through the jump rings to secure them in place to the crocheted project.

## HOT GLUE GUN

Apply the hot glue to the back of the applique first, then set it upon the crocheted piece, holding it down for a few seconds to allow the glue to cool and secure in place.

## FABRIC LINING A PROJECT

Measure out the fabric, aligning with the finished crochet project, allowing a decrease within a few centimeters to cut the fabric. Align the crochet edges with the fabric. Use a hot glue gun or needle and matching thread to sew the fabric to the inside of the crochet project.

## SEWING

Thread your sewing needle. Work from the inside of your project and through the crochet stitches to attach the band. Secure in place by sewing the two notions together.

# CROCHET CLOTHING CONSTRUCTION

## WORKING IN PANELS

When constructing crochet tops, they will be formed with two main panels [front and back].

## CREATING THE SHOULDERS

The shoulders are formed at the very last row. At the top of the crocheted panel, leave the middle stitches free for the neckline. Reinsert your hook into the same row [opposite side] once one set of shoulder rows is complete.

## CUSTOMIZATIONS

The best part of creating your own clothing is the opportunity to customize and construct the handmade project in the way you would like it. The designs are easily adjustable; freely open to add or alter the way you would truly love to see it.

# CREATING ARMHOLE/SLEEVE OPENINGS

## METHOD #1

Construct the sleeves by skipping 2 STS and reinserting your hook into the third stitch, crocheting the rest of the row until you reach the third last stitch. Turn piece to continue work. Omit 4 TOTAL stitches (2 stitches at each end) to construct the sleeve openings.

## METHOD #2

Constructing the sleeves, insert your hook into the top side of the crocheted piece, working vertically along the edge to create your sleeve openings.

# CHANGING COLORS

## METHOD #1

Working primarily at the end of the completed row, when you're changing colors (example: creating stripes), you will keep the first color you have on your hook and place the new color onto the crochet hook. Pull the secondary/new color through the first/old color's two loops, then you'll turn your project at the end of the row. Utilizing the turning chain method, apply the appropriate chains and continue work.

# METHOD #2

When working with graphs, switch colors as you follow each color square as they appear. Each color change can be created within the same row more than once to create the graphic. Before approaching the last stitch before a color change, following METHOD ONE, place the new color onto the crochet hook and work the appropriate technique into that last stitch, pull through the new color from the two loops to create the color change.

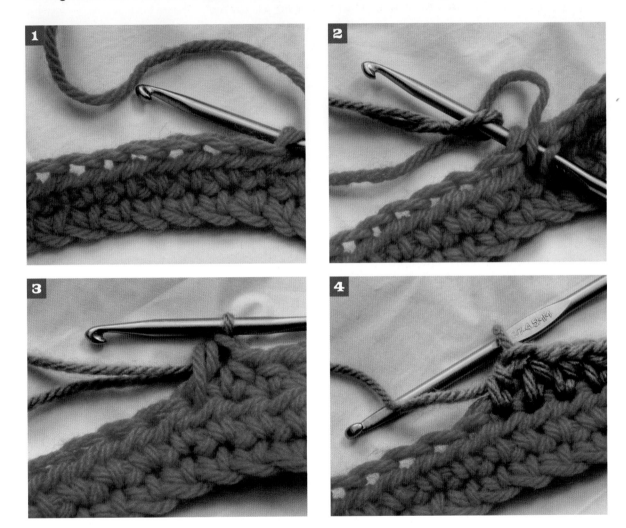

## IMPLEMENTING SUSPENDER CLIPS

Guide the crocheted strap through the band using the tapestry yarn sewing needle and threading a strand of yarn. Overlap the crochet strap and sew, securing the strap and suspender clip in place.

# CROCHET BLOCKING

Blocking your crochet is a process used to form and shape your work. Block the designated pieces right before proceeding to the seaming together step to construct the specific measurements.

## METHOD #1

Lay the piece on a foam core board or blocking board. Following the specific measurements, use rust proof T-pins to pin the piece to the board. Spray the piece lightly with a water bottle or fully immerse it in water. Allow piece to air dry.

## METHOD #2

Lay the piece on a foam core board or blocking board. Following the specific measurements, use rust-proof T-pins to pin the piece to the board. Gently apply heat or steam lightly to shape your work. Depending on the fiber content of the yarn, place a protective barrier such as a towel on the piece to protect it from scorching.

# THE
# 1970s

The 1970s was before my time, but the era still greatly influenced me. So many important events took place that brought cultural and social change, continuing the momentum from the 1960s and taking it to another level. More women were joining the workforce and stepping out into the forefront (the freeze-frame of Mary Tyler Moore throwing her hat comes to mind) and activists working to move the country forward through music, art, and social movements. It was an inspiring time. Disco was the soundtrack of this era; *Saturday Night Fever* and Donna Summer colored the '70s as a joyous representation of life and self-expression.

## FAVORITE MOVIES

- *Planet of the Apes*
- *Star Wars*
- *Foxy Brown*

## FAVORITE TV SHOWS

- *Wonder Woman*
- *Good Times*
- *Josie and the Pussycats*

## OTHER FAVORITE THINGS

- The Civil Rights and Women's Rights movements
- Disco
- Mood rings

## ICONS OF THE ERA

- Shirley Chisholm
- David Bowie
- Diana Ross

# SMILEY CROCHET EARRINGS

This bright and happy drop earring is inspired by the enduring symbol of positivity and revolution. It has found new lives throughout the times, and its genre-defying accessibility works well with multiple styles, from tie-dye psychedelic looks to rave culture-inspired fashion.

## MATERIALS

YARN: Red Heart Super Saver; 100% Acrylic (364 yards/198 meters); medium #4 Saffron (Color A), Black (Color B): 1 skein each (project used less than half each skein)

HOOK: US size 7 (4.5mm) crochet hook

EXTRAS: 1 [9 × 12] felt square (yellow), 2 gold metal earrings, 2 gold metal jump rings, craft scissors, measuring tape, fabric glue or hot glue gun, fabric pen, pliers (to open the jump rings), yarn needle

GAUGE: 3 ROUNDS = 3.5" in pattern

# THE PATTERN

The earrings are worked in rounds, starting with the face. Create two round pieces for each earring, then join them together. The features (eyes and smiles) are crocheted separately and sewn onto the face pieces.

## CREATING THE FACE

**Note:** You will repeat this step two times to create TWO pieces, using Color A.

CH 3, SL ST to connect the last ST to the very first ST, creating a mini circle.

**RND1:** CH 2 (does count as first HDC), then into the middle of the circle, HDC 8 times, to create your first round. At the end of the round, SL ST to connect and continue work. [8 HDC TOTAL]

**RND2:** CH 2, then into each ST, HDC TWO times, to create your second round. At the end of the round, SL ST to connect and continue work. [16 HDC TOTAL]

**RND3:** CH 2, then HDC in the next ST and HDC TWO times into every 2nd ST, to create the third round. At the end of the round, SL ST to complete work. [24 HDC TOTAL]

Fasten off. Weave in ends.

## CREATING THE EYES

**Note:** You will repeat this step for a total of FOUR pieces to create two sets of eyes.

Use Color B.

CH 3, SL ST to connect the last ST to the very first ST, creating a mini circle.

**RND1:** CH 2 (does count as first HDC), then into the middle of the circle, HDC 8 times, to create your first round. At the end of the round, SL ST to connect. Fasten off. Weave in ends.

## CREATING THE SMILE

**Note:** You will repeat this step TWICE.

Use Color A.

CH 9. Fasten off. Weave in ends.

## PLACING THE EYES

Apply fabric adhesive to the back of the eyes. Place the eyes onto the front of the face, at the second round of the face two STS apart.

## PLACING THE SMILE

Underneath the set of eyes (at the fifth chain ST), set the smile in the middle of the face, half circling the piece.

## CREATING THE DANGLING CHAIN

Note: You will repeat this step TWICE.

Using Color A.

Insert the hook into the top of the face above the eyes into the last round.

CH 8. Fasten off. Weave in ends.

## PLACING THE METAL JUMP RINGS

With the pliers, open the metal jump rings. Slide the opening through the last dangling yarn chain crocheted and connect. Then, with the metal earring, clasp the metal ring close to secure both the metal earrings and the crochet dangling chain.

## ADDING THE FELT

Note: Repeat this step a total of TWO times for both individual rounds.

Place the face round onto the felt square. Trace around the face with your felt pen and cut out the felt circle. Then, use your fabric glue or hot glue gun to apply the cut felt round to the BACK of the face round, securing it in place.

# THE GROOVY CROCHET SKIRT

Ride the wave fantastic in this retro skirt. Following the curved patterns of the 1970s, this item consists of four repeating colors that feel fun, free, and yet structured at the same time. Dress it up with a fitted turtleneck, or dress it down with equally groovy tees.

## MATERIALS

YARN: Red Heart Super Saver; 100% Acrylic (364 yards/198 meters); medium #4
Amethyst (Color A), Gold (Color B), Carrot (Color C), Flamingo (Color D): 1 skein each (project used less than half each skein)
Big Twist Yarns; 100% Acrylic (380 yards/ 170 meters); medium #4
Magenta (Color E): 1 skein (project used less than half each skein)

HOOK: US size 7 (4.5mm) crochet hook

EXTRAS: craft scissors, measuring tape, fabric glue or hot glue gun, sewing needle sewing thread, yarn needle, 2 safety pins, sewing needle, matching thread, Dritz ½" Braided Elastic 4-½ yards

GAUGE: 11 STS/6 DC ROWS = 4"

## MEASUREMENTS

13.5+ inches length

## SIZING

SM: [26 inches width]

MD: [35 inches width]

LG/1XL: [43.5 inches width]

2XL/3XL: [52 inches width]

4XL/5XL: [61 inches width]

# THE PATTERN

The skirt begins with the waistband. The waistband is worked flat, seamed, and the elastic band added. Complete the waistband, then work the skirt in the round from the top down.

## CROCHET WAISTBAND

Crochet a horizontal piece that will be sewn around the elastic band.

With Color A, CH 72 (96, 120, 144, 168).

**ROW1-ROW4:** [Color A] Alternate between SC and HDC into all the STS for ALL the rows [R1 = SC, R2 = HDC, R3 = SC, R4 = HDC], turn work when complete. Once you've completed R4, fasten off and weave in the ends.

## CUT ELASTIC

### Elastic Band Measurements

Cut a half inch more of the elastic than the crochet waistband measurement so that the elastic band overlaps when sewn together.

SM: [26.5 inches width]

MD: [35.5 inches width]

LG/1XL: [44 inches width]

2XL/3XL: [52.5 inches width]

4XL/5XL: [61.5 inches width]

Fold the horizontal crochet waistband piece entirely in half. Thread Color A to sew the folded crochet piece together. Leave the sides of the waistband piece open so that the elastic can go through. Cut the yarn and weave in the ends.

## INSERT ELASTIC

With the safety pin, attach to the elastic. Guide the elastic through the crochet waistband. Scrunch to guide the elastic through the crocheted band. Once it is in accordingly, thread your sewing needle with matching thread, overlap the elastic ends together for a snug fit, and sew the elastic together.

**Note:** Make sure it is sewn tightly for security! Cut thread and knot.

# BOTTOM OF SKIRT

This step is to start the BOTTOM of the skirt. Work in rounds to construct the skirt by inserting your hook into the stitch of the crocheted waistband.

SM: 72 STS [26 inches width]

MD: 96 STS [35 inches width]

LG/1XL: 120 STS [43.5 inches width]

2XL/3XL: 144 STS [52 inches width]

4XL/5XL: 168 STS [61 inches width]

[Color A] Join with SL ST, CH 3 (counts as first DC), DC around for 72 (96, 120, 144, 168) STS. Join with a SL ST to the beginning CH.

**RND1:** [Color A] CH 3, 2 DC in the same ST, *SK next 2 STS, 3 DC all in the next ST, SK next 2 STS, 3 DC all in the next ST, SK next 2 STS, (3 DC, CH 3, 3 DC) all in the next ST, SK next 2 STS, 3 DC all in the next ST, SK next 2 STS, 3 DC all in the next ST, SK next 2 STS, 3 DC in the next ST, SK next 5 STS, 3 DC in the next ST; repeat from * around until 5 STS remain, SK the last 5 STS, join with a SL ST to the beginning CH.

Note: When indicated to work in the space in between the 3 DC CLUSTERS, work the 3 DC STS in the space.

**RND2:** [Color D] SL ST in the next 2 DC, SL ST in the space in between the 3 DC CLUSTER, CH 3, 2 DC in the same space, *SK the next 3 DC, 3 DC in the space in between the CLUSTERS, SK 3 DC, in the CH 3 space from the previous row (3 DC, CH 3, 3 DC) all in the same space, SK 3 DC, 3 DC in the next space in between the CLUSTERS, SK 3 DC, 3 DC in the next space in between the 3 DC CLUSTERS, SK 3 DC, 3 DC in the next space in between the 3 DC CLUSTERS, SK the next 6 DC (TWO 3 DC CLUSTERS), 3 DC in the next space in between the 3 DC CLUSTERS; repeat from * around, join with a SL ST to the beginning CH.

**RND3:** [Color E] SL ST in the next 2 DC, SL ST in the space in between the 3 DC CLUSTER, CH 3, 2 DC in the same space, *SK the next 3 DC, 3 DC in the space in between the CLUSTERS, SK 3 DC, in the CH 3 space from the previous row (3 DC, CH 3, 3 DC) all in the same space, SK 3 DC, 3 DC in the next space in between the CLUSTERS, SK 3 DC, 3 DC in the next space in between the 3 DC CLUSTERS, SK 3 DC, 3 DC in the next space in between the 3 DC CLUSTERS, SK the next 6 DC (TWO 3 DC CLUSTERS), 3 DC in the next space in between the 3 DC CLUSTERS; repeat from * around, join with a SL ST to the beginning CH.

**RND4:** [Color C] SL ST in the next 2 DC, SL ST in the space in between the 3 DC CLUSTER, CH 3, 2 DC in the same space, *SK the next 3 DC, 3 DC in the space in between the CLUSTERS, SK 3 DC, in the CH 3 space from the previous row (3 DC, CH 3, 3 DC) all in the same space, SK 3 DC, 3 DC in the next space in between the CLUSTERS, SK 3 DC, 3 DC in the next space in between the 3 DC CLUSTERS, SK 3 DC, 3 DC in the next space in between the 3 DC CLUSTERS, SK the next 6 DC (TWO 3 DC CLUSTERS), 3 DC in the next space in between the 3 DC CLUSTERS; repeat from * around, join with a SL ST to the beginning CH.

Continue working every round in the established pattern (repeat RND4), changing colors following the sequence below:

**RND5:** [Color B]

**RND6:** [Color A]

**RND7:** [Color D]

**RND8:** [Color E]

**RND9:** [Color C]

**RND10:** [Color B]

**RND11-RND12:** [Color A]

**RND13:** [Color D]

**RND14:** [Color E]

**RND15:** [Color C]

**RND16:** [Color B]

**RND17-RND18:** [Color A]

**RND19:** [Color A] CH 1, SC around and into all the 72 (96, 120, 144, 168) STS for the entire round, join with a SL ST to complete final work. Fasten off. Weave in ends.

**Note:** For personal desired length, continue adding rounds, maintaining established color sequence.

The 1970s

# THE JIVIN' CROCHET SKIRT

Jumpers are a favorite of mine; they scream 1970s fashion. I've taken the classic concept with its two straps attached by metal suspender clips and embellished it with a line of flowers across the waist. Be bold and choose your favorite color combinations!

## MATERIALS

YARN: Red Heart Super Saver; 100% Acrylic (364 yards/198 meters); medium #4
Gold: 2 skeins

HOOK: US size 7 (4.5mm) crochet hook

EXTRAS: 2 sets of 2 suspender clips, 1 button [2 cm], craft scissors, measuring tape, fabric glue or hot glue gun, sewing needle, matching thread, yarn needle, 6-8 retro floral appliques

WAISTBAND GAUGE: 9 HDC STS = 4" & 2.5" width

BOTTOM SKIRT GAUGE: 11 HDC STS/ 6 DC ROWS = 4"

## MEASUREMENTS

14 inches length [excluding suspenders]

## SIZING

XS: [23 inches width]

SM: [28 inches width]

MD: [32 inches width]

LG/1XL: [38 inches width]

2XL/3XL: [44 inches width]

4XL/5XL: [50 inches width]

# THE PATTERN

The skirt begins with the waistband. The waistband is worked flat, seamed. Complete the waistband, then work the skirt in the round from the top down. Finish with the suspenders.

## STARTING THE WAISTBAND OF THE SKIRT

CH 5 [to 2.5 inches width] to create one long crocheted band.

XS: 57 ROWS [23 inches width]

SMALL: 69 ROWS STS [28 inches width]

MEDIUM: 81 ROWS [32 inches width]

LG/1XL: 96 ROWS [38 inches width]

2XL/3XL: 111 ROWS [44 inches width]

4XL/5XL: 125 ROWS [50 inches width]

**R1:** CH 1, SK 1 CH, SC into all the chs for the row. At the end of the row, turn work after completion.

**R2: CREATE THE BUTTONHOLE:** CH 2, HDC into the first 2 STS, CH 1, SK 1 ST and HDC in all the remaining STS, turn work after completion.

**Note:** On the next row, work a ST into the CH 1 space.

**R3-R57 // R69 // R81 // R96 // R111 // R125:** Alternate between SC and HDC into all the STS for ALL the rows [EX: R3 = SC & R4 = HDC], turn work when complete. SL ST, fasten off work. Weave in ends.

Rejoin the hook into the top side stitch of the band. SC once along the top of the completed band. At the end of the row, fasten off work and weave in the ends. Then, reinsert the hook into the bottom side stitch and SC once along the bottom of the band. At the end of the row, fasten off work and weave in the ends.

## CONNECTING THE BAND

Using the yarn needle and a strand of yarn, overlap the band's first and last rows vertically to sew the bottom together to secure and create a round crocheted piece.

## STARTING THE BOTTOM OF THE SKIRT

Work from the bottom row of the crocheted waistband in rounds. Attach yarn with a SL ST after every completed round.

**RND1:** CH 2, HDC into all the STS for the entire round. At the end of the round, SL ST to continue work. [57 (69, 81, 96, 111, 125) STS]

**RND2:** CH 3, DC into the first ST and *into the next ST (DC TWO TIMES) all into the SAME ST, then DC into the next ST; repeat from * until the end of the round. At the end of the round, SL ST to continue work. [85 (69, 103, 144, 166, 189) STS]

Note: Extend rounds within this section, for personal desired length.

**RND3-RND12:** CH 3, DC into all the STS for all the rounds. At the end of each round, SL ST to continue work. At the final round, SL ST to complete final work. Fasten off. Weave in ends.

## MAKE THE SUSPENDERS

Note: Repeat this step for a total of TWO times for a pair of suspenders.

22.5 inches length

CH 68 [extend/decrease to desired length]

**R1:** CH 2, HDC into all the STS across row. When the row is complete, SL ST. Fasten off work, weave in ends.

## ATTACHING THE SUSPENDER CLIPS

Wrap the suspender clip through the end of the strap, overlapping it over the metal clip. Use the yarn needle and a strand of yarn to secure the clip.

## ATTACHING THE BUTTON

Use the yarn sewing needle and a strand of yarn to secure the button to the waistband. Secure the button at the opposite middle position of where the buttonhole was constructed at the end of the final middle row from when creating the waistband.

## ADDING THE FLORAL APPLIQUES

Using fabric adhesive or hot glue gun, apply glue to the back of the appliques to set upon the waistband of the skirt. Hold firmly to secure for a few seconds. Place floral appliques however you personally desire!

Using a sewing needle and matching thread, insert the needle into the edge of the applique to sew around the edge of the applique onto the crocheted band. Weave in any remaining ends.

# THE POWER FLOWER CROCHET BAG

When you're capturing the spirit of the 1970s, you can never have enough floral print. The big flower design on both sides makes this a statement bag despite its effortlessly casual style. This long-strapped bag can be worn over the shoulder or across the body.

## MATERIALS

YARN: Red Heart Super Saver; 100% Acrylic (364 yards/198 meters); medium #4 Pretty In Pink (Color A), Medium Purple (Color B), Bright Yellow (Color C): 1 skein each (project used less than half each skein)

HOOK: US size 7 (4.5mm) crochet hook

EXTRAS: 1 [9 × 12] felt square (pink), craft scissors, measuring tape, fabric glue or hot glue gun, sewing needle, matching thread, fabric pen, yarn needle

GAUGE: 11 HDC STS/10 HDC ROWS = 4"

## MEASUREMENTS

7.5 inches length × 8.5 inches width

# THE PATTERN

The bag is worked flat with the graphic on the front panel and the back left plain.

### STARTING THE PROJECT

CH 21.

**R1:** [Color A] CH 2. (Turning Chain at the beginning of the row, does not count as a ST.) HDC into all of the STS for the entire row. At the end of the row, turn work to continue.

**FROM LEFT SIDE: R2:** [Color A] CH 2, HDC 6 STS---[Color B] HDC 2 STS---[Color A] HDC 13 STS. At the end of the row, turn work to continue.

**RIGHT SIDE: R3:** [Color A] CH 2, HDC 5 STS---[Color B] HDC 3 STS---[Color A] HDC 4 STS---[Color B] HDC 5 STS---[Color A] HDC 4 STS. At the end of the row, turn work to continue.

**LEFT SIDE: R4:** [Color A] CH 2, HDC 4 STS---[Color B] HDC 6 STS---[Color A] HDC 2 STS---[Color B] HDC 5 STS---[Color A] HDC 4 STS. At the end of the row, turn work to continue.

**RIGHT SIDE: R5:** [Color A] CH 2, HDC 4 STS---[Color B] HDC 13 STS---[Color A] HDC 4 STS. At the end of the row, turn work to continue.

**LEFT SIDE: R6:** [Color A] CH 2, HDC 4 STS---[Color B] HDC 13 STS---[Color A] HDC 4 STS. At the end of the row, turn work to continue.

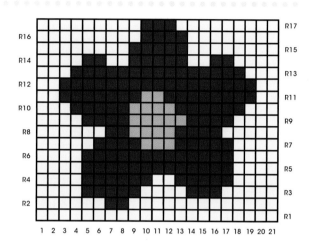

**RIGHT SIDE: R7:** [Color A] CH 2, HDC 4 STS---[Color B] HDC 5 STS---[Color C] HDC 3 STS---[Color B] HDC 4 STS---[Color A] HDC 5 STS. At the end of the row, turn work to continue.

**LEFT SIDE: R8:** [Color A] CH 2, HDC 6 STS---[Color B] HDC 2 STS---[Color C] HDC 4 STS---[Color B] HDC 4 STS---[Color A] HDC 5 STS. At the end of the row, turn work to continue.

**RIGHT SIDE: R9:** [Color A] CH 2, HDC 4 STS---[Color B] HDC 4 STS---[Color C] HDC 5 STS---[Color B] HDC 4 STS---[Color A] HDC 4 STS. At the end of the row, turn work to continue.

**LEFT SIDE: R10:** [Color A] CH 2, HDC 3 STS---[Color B] HDC 5 STS---[Color C] HDC 4 STS---[Color B] HDC 6 STS---[Color A] HDC 3 STS. At the end of the row, turn work to continue.

**RIGHT SIDE: R11:** [Color A] CH 2, HDC 2 STS---[Color B] HDC 8 STS---[Color C] HDC 2 STS---[Color B] HDC 7 STS---[Color A] HDC 2 STS. At the end of the row, turn work to continue.

**LEFT SIDE: R12:** [Color A] CH 2, HDC 2 STS---[Color B] HDC 17 STS---[Color A] HDC 2 STS. At the end of the row, turn work to continue.

**RIGHT SIDE: R13:** [Color A] CH 2, HDC 3 STS---[Color B] HDC 15 STS---[Color A] HDC 3 STS. At the end of the row, turn work to continue.

**LEFT SIDE: R14:** [Color A] CH 2, HDC 4 STS---[Color B] HDC 2 STS---[Color A] HDC 2 STS---[Color B] HDC 5 STS---[Color A] HDC 2 STS---[Color B] HDC 2 STS---[Color A] HDC 4 STS. At the end of the row, turn work to continue.

**RIGHT SIDE: R15:** [Color A] CH 2, HDC 8 STS---[Color B] HDC 5 STS---[Color A] HDC 8 STS. At the end of the row, turn work to continue.

**LEFT SIDE: R16:** [Color A] CH 2, HDC 9 STS---[Color B] HDC 4 STS---[Color A] HDC 8 STS. At the end of the row, turn work to continue.

**RIGHT SIDE: R17:** [Color A] CH 2, HDC 9 STS---[Color B] HDC 3 STS---[Color A] HDC 9 STS. At the end of the row, turn work to continue.

**LEFT SIDE: R18:** [Color A] CH 1, SC into all the STS for the entire row. At the end of the row, turn work to continue.

**Note:** For Finishing Technique: CH 1, SC around the entire finished piece once with 3 SC in each corner. At the end of the round, SL ST at the end of the round to complete final work. Fasten off. Weave in ends.

## CREATING THE BACK PANEL FOR THE BAG

CH 21.

**R1:** [Color A] CH 2, SK 2, HDC into all of the CH for the row. At the end of each row, turn work to continue.

**R2-R17:** [Color A] CH 2, HDC into all of the STS for all of the rows. At the end of each row, turn work to continue.

**R18:** [Color A] CH 1, SC into all of the STS for the entire row. At the end of the row, SL ST to complete work for this section.

Note: For finishing technique: CH 1, SC around the entire finished piece once with 3 SC in each corner. At the end of the round, SL ST to complete final work. Fasten off. Weave in ends.

## ATTACHING THE FABRIC LINING

Cut two sets of fabric from the fat square. Cut around the finished crochet FRONT AND BACK PANEL pieces a little less than 7.5 inches length × 7.25 inches width. Sew or utilize fabric glue adhesive to apply the fabric to the back of the finished crochet pieces.

## SEWING THE BACK AND FRONT PANELS TOGETHER

Next, use the yarn needle and three sets of a long strand of Color A to sew both vertical sides and the horizontal bottom of the bag, FRONT AND BACK together, leaving the top open.

## CREATING THE STRAPS

CH 50, CH 2, SK 2, HDC for one row to create the strap. At the end of the row, SL ST to complete work.

Next, using the yarn needle and two sets of a long strand of Color A, sew each strap [LEFT AND RIGHT CORNER SIDES] to the TOP sides of the bag [R18]. Fasten off. Weave in ends.

# THE RAINBOW BELLE CROCHET TOP

There's no way you won't feel like a showstopper in this hippie-chic look. With exaggerated bell sleeves and an assortment of prominent colors throughout, this eclectic sweater will undoubtedly be the focal point of your outfit. I like pairing it with classic staples like denim or a black skirt to really let all the colors shine.

## MATERIALS

**YARN:** Loops & Threads Impeccable Ombre Yarn; 100% Acrylic (187 yards/171 meters); medium #4
Rainbow: 4 skeins

**HOOK:** US size 7 (4.5mm) crochet hook

**EXTRAS:** craft scissors, measuring tape, yarn needle

**GAUGE:** 11 HDC STS/6 DC ROWS = 4"

## SIZING

SM/MD: [32 inches]

LG/XL: [44 inches]

2XL/3XL: [51 inches]

4XL/5XL: [59 inches]

# THE PATTERN

The top begins with granny squares for the front and back panels. The panels are seamed together, and then the sleeves are worked from the shoulder to the cuff. Adjust the length to your desired fit.

## CREATING THE GRANNY SQUARE

Create two large granny square crocheted pieces for the FRONT AND BACK panels for the top.

Work in rounds.

CH 4 and connect with a SL ST, insert hook into the circle to work in the round.

**RND1:** CH 3 (counts as the first DC), insert hook into the circle to work in the round, make 2 DC, CH 3, (3 DC, CH 3) THREE times. Join with a SL ST at the top first ST of the starting CH 3. [12 DC, 4 CH-3]

**RND2:** CH 4 (counts as the first DC and CH 1 corner space), *into the next CH 3 space, make 3 DC, CH 3, 3 DC, CH 1; repeat from * TWO times for a total of 3 times around. Now, into the last CH 3 space, make (3 DC, CH 3, 2 DC), join with a SL ST to the 3rd CH of the starting CH.

**RND3:** CH 3 (counts as the first DC), into the next CH 1 space, work 2 DC, CH 1, *into the following CH 3 corner space, make (3 DC, CH 3, 3 DC, CH 1), then into the next CH 1 space make (3 DC, CH 1) across to the next corner; repeat from * all around until you reach the beginning CH. Then, join with a SL ST to the top starting CH 3.

**RND4:** CH 4 counts as the first DC and CH 1 space), *into the next CH 1 space, make (3 DC, CH 1) across to the next corner, into the following CH 3 corner space, make (3 DC, CH 3, 3 DC, CH 1); repeat from * all around, into the last CH 1 space, make 2 DC. Join with a SL ST to the top of starting CH 3.

## TO INCREASE SQUARE

Repeat methods of RND3 and RND4 to desired sizing. Do not fasten off the last round.

SM/MD: ROUND 13

LG/XL: ROUND 19

2XL/3XL: ROUND 22

4XL/5XL: ROUND 26

## CREATING THE SLEEVES

Turn the square to work horizontally along the side of the square to create the sleeves.

**Note:** You will repeat this step FOUR times total (TWICE for each side of the crocheted piece).

SM/MD: 15 STS

LG/XL: 18 STS

2XL/3XL: 21 STS

4XL/5XL: 24 STS

**R1:** CH 2, HDC into 15 (18, 21, 24) STS for the entire row, working in between the CH 1 as well. At the end of the row, turn to continue work.

**R2:** CH 2, HDC all STS for the entire row. At the end of the row, fasten off.

## SEWING THE TOP TOGETHER

This step is to sew the crocheted pieces together to create your top. Lay both completed pieces flat. Now, sew the sides together using the yarn needle and yarn, leaving the ARMHOLE sections completely open.

## SEWING THE NECKLINE TOGETHER

This step is to sew the shoulders for the left and right sides.

Using the yarn needle and a strand of yarn, this step will be repeated TWICE for both sides of the neck to form the neckline at the top row.

SEWING SHOULDERS SIZES (adjust to your personal desire).

SM/MD: 8 STS

2XL/3XL: 18 STS

LG/XL: 12 STS

4XL/5XL: 20 STS

## FORMING THE SLEEVES

Working in rounds, join with a SL ST to connect. Insert hook into the armholes where the HDC ROWS were formed. This step will be repeated for BOTH LEFT AND RIGHT ARMHOLE SIDES.

**RND1:** CH 3, DC into the first ST, CH 1, SK 2 STS, *(DC THREE TIMES) all into the SAME ST, CH 1, SK 2 STS; repeat from * until the end of the round. At the end of the round, SL ST to continue work.

**RND2-RND12:** CH 4, TRC into the first ST, CH 1, *into the space formed by the CH 1 of the previous round, (TRC THREE TIMES) all into the SAME space, SK 3 STS, CH 1; repeat from * working into CH 1 space until the end of the round. At the end of the round, SL ST continue work.

**RND13:** CH 4, TRC into the first ST, CH 1, *into the space formed by the CH 1 of the previous round, (TRC TWO TIMES, CH 1, TRC TWO TIMES) all into the SAME space, SK 2 STS, CH 1; repeat from * working into CH 1 space until the end of the round. At the end of the round, SL ST continue work.

**RND14:** CH 4, TRC into the first ST, CH 2, *into the space formed by the CH 1 of the previous round, [TRC TWO TIMES, CH 2, TRC TWO TIMES] all into the SAME space, SK 2 STS, CH 3; repeat from * working into CH 1 space until the end of the round. At the end of the round, SL ST continue work.

**RND15-RND21:** CH 4, TRC into the first ST, CH 3, *into the space formed by the CH 2 of the previous round, (TRC TWO TIMES, CH 3, TRC TWO TIMES) all into the SAME space, SK 2 STS, CH 1; repeat from * working into CH 1 space until the end of the round. At the end of the round, SL ST continue work.

**Note:** Extend rounds here for personal desired length before moving onto the final round!

**RND22 [FINAL RND]:** CH 4, TRC into the first ST, CH 4, *into the space formed by the CH 3 of the previous round (TRC FIVE TIMES, CH 4, TRC FIVE TIMES) all into the SAME space, SK 2 STS, CH 4; repeat from * working into CH 1 space until the end of the round. At the end of the final round, fasten off. Weave in ends.

# THE OUT OF SIGHT CROCHET BAG

Keep it all the way 70's with this granny square crochet bag! The vintage handmade style is inspired by the handcrafted and free loving time.

## MATERIALS

YARN: Red Heart Super Saver; 100% Acrylic (364 yards/198 meters); medium #4 Cherry Red (Color A), Aran (Color B) Bright Yellow (Color C), Pumpkin (Color D), Royal (Color E): 1 skein each (project used less than half each skein)

HOOK: US size 7 (4.5mm) crochet hook

EXTRAS: 2 [9 × 12] felt squares or 2 Fabric Fat Squares (Red), craft scissors, measuring tape, fabric glue or hot glue gun, needle and thread, fabric pen, yarn needle, 1 [47 inch] metal purse chain strap, 2 metal jump rings, jewelry pliers (to open the jump rings)

GAUGE: Not necessary for project

## MEASUREMENTS

8.5 inches length × 8.5 inches width

# THE PATTERN

## CREATING THE FRONT GRANNY SQUARE

**RND1:** [Color E] CH 4 and connect with a SL ST, insert hook into the circle to work in the round.

CH 3 (counts as the first DC), make 2 DC, CH 3, (3 DC, CH 3) THREE TIMES. Join with a SL ST at the top first ST of the starting CH 3.

**RND2:** [Color C] CH 4 (counts as the first DC and CH 1 corner space), *into the next CH 3 space, make (3 DC, CH 3, 3 DC), CH 1, SK next 3 DC; repeat from * around into the next TWO CH 3 spaces. Now, into the last CH 3 space, (3 DC, CH 3, 2 DC). Join with a SL ST to the 3rd CH of the starting CH 4.

**RND3:** [Color D] CH 3 (counts as the first DC), into the next CH 1 space, make 2 DC, CH 1, SK 3 DC, *into the next CH 3 corner space, make (3 DC, CH 3, 3 DC), CH 1, SK 3 DC, 3 DC into the next CH 1 space, CH 1; repeat from * around until you reach the last CH 3 corner space, in the last CH 3 corner space, make (3 DC, CH 3, 3 DC), CH 1. Join with a SL ST in the 3rd CH of the starting CH 3.

**RND4:** [Color B] CH 4 (counts as the first DC and CH 1 space), 3 DC in the next CH 1 space, CH 1, SK 3 DC, *into the next CH 3 corner space, make (3 DC STS, CH 3, 3 DC STS), (CH 1, SK 3 DC, 3 DC in next CH 1 space) TWO TIMES across to next CH 3 corner space; repeat from * around until the last CH 1 space. Into the last CH 1 space, make 2 DC. Join with a SL ST to the 3rd CH of the starting CH 4.

**RND5:** [Color A] CH 3 (counts as the first DC), into the next CH 1 space, make 2 DC, CH 1, (SK 3 DC, 3 DC in the next CH 1 space, CH 1) across to next CH 3 corner space, *into the following CH 3 corner space, make (3 DC, CH 3, 3 DC), (CH 1, SK 3 DC, into the next CH 1 space make 3 DC, CH 1) THREE TIMES to the next CH 3 corner space; repeat from * around until you reach the beginning CH. Join with a SL ST to the 3rd CH of the starting CH 3.

**RND6:** [Color A] CH 4 (counts as the first DC and CH 1 space), (into the next CH 1 space, make 3 DC, CH 1) TWO TIMES, *into the next CH 3 corner space, make (3 DC, CH 3, 3 DC), CH 1, (into the next CH 1 space make 3 DC, CH 1) FOUR TIMES; repeat from * until you reach the last CH 1 space. Into the last CH 1 space make 2 DC. Join with a SL ST to the 3rd CH of the starting CH 4 to complete work. Fasten off. Weave in ends.

## CREATING THE BACK GRANNY SQUARE

**RND1:** [Color A] CH 4 and connect with a SL ST, insert hook into the circle to work in the round.

CH 3 (counts as the first DC), make 2 DC, CH 3, (3 DC, CH 3) THREE TIMES. Join with a SL ST at the top first ST of the starting CH 3.

**RND2:** [Color A] CH 4 (counts as the first DC and CH 1 corner space), *into the next CH 3 space, make (3 DC, CH 3, 3 DC), CH 1, SK next 3 DC; repeat from * around into the next TWO CH 3 spaces. Now, into the last CH 3 space, make (3 DC, CH 3, 2 DC). Join with a SL ST to the 3rd CH of the starting CH 4.

**RND3:** [Color A] CH 3 (counts as the first DC), into the next CH 1 space, make 2 DC, CH 1, SK 3 DC, *into the next CH 3 corner space, make (3 DC, CH 3, 3 DC), CH 1, SK 3 DC, into the next CH 1 space 3 DC, CH 1; repeat from * around until you reach the last CH 3 corner space, in the last CH 3 corner space, make (3 DC, CH 3, 3 DC), CH 1. Join with a SL ST in the 3rd CH of the starting CH 3.

**RND4:** [Color A] CH 4 (counts as the first DC and CH 1 space), 3 DC in the next CH 1 space, CH 1, SK 3 DC, *into the next CH 3 corner space, make (3 DC, CH 3, 3 DC), (CH 1, SK 3 DC, 3 DC in next CH 1 space) TWO TIMES across to next CH 3 corner space; repeat from * around until the last CH 1 space. Into the last CH 1 space, make 2 DC. Join with a SL ST to the 3rd CH of the starting CH 4.

**RND5:** [Color A] CH 3 (counts as the first DC), into the next CH 1 space, make 2 DC, CH 1, (SK 3 DC, 3 DC in the next CH 1 space, CH 1) across to next CH 3 corner space, *into the following CH 3 corner space, make (3 DC, CH 3, 3 DC), (CH 1, SK 3 DC, into the next CH 1 space make 3 DC, CH 1) THREE TIMES to the next CH 3 corner space; repeat from * around until you reach the beginning CH. Join with a SL ST to the 3rd CH of the starting CH 3.

**RND6:** (Color A) CH 4 (counts as the first DC and CH 1 space), (into the next CH 1 space, make 3 DC, CH 1) TWO TIMES, *into the next CH 3 corner space, make (3 DC, CH 3, 3 DC), CH 1, (into the next CH 1 space make 3 DC, CH 1) FOUR TIMES; repeat from * until you reach the last CH 1 space. Into the last CH 1 space make 2 DC. Join with a SL ST to the 3rd CH of the starting CH 4 to complete work. Fasten off. Weave in ends.

## ATTACHING THE FABRIC LINING

Cut 2 SETS of fabric from the fat square or felt square to the measurements of the finished crochet FRONT AND BACK PANEL pieces a little less than [8.5 inches length × 8.25 inches width]. Either sew or utilize fabric glue adhesive, apply to the back of the finished crochet pieces to secure it in place.

## SEWING THE BACK AND FRONT PANELS TOGETHER

Next, utilizing your yarn sewing needle and 3 SETS of a long strand of Color A, sew both vertical sides and the bottom of the bag, FRONT AND BACK together, leaving the top open.

## ATTACHING THE METAL JUMP RINGS

Using the jewelry pliers, open the metal jump ring, guide the jump ring through the top side corner of the bag. Repeat for the other side of the bag.

## ATTACHING THE PURSE STRAP

Opening the clasp, guide the purse strap through the metal jump ring, enclosing both rings for each side.

# THE
# 1980s

This decade was the true beginning of pop culture as we know it today. MTV revolutionized the way people consumed media. Madonna, Prince, and Michael Jackson were like royalty, and so many more artists took the world by storm with their bold creativity that got people thinking and talking. The music of this decade feels beyond its time and proves that you could change the world if you were outrageously talented. My favorite movie of all time, *Willow*, came out during this era, so it holds a special place in my heart. If you've never seen it, *Willow* is a beautiful fantasy movie directed by Ron Howard with the message that the power we need exists within us. This notion has stuck with me to this day.

## FAVORITE MOVIES

- *Willow*
- *E.T.*
- *Splash*

## FAVORITE TV SHOWS

- *She-Ra: The Princess of Power*
- *A Different World*
- *Growing Pains*

## OTHER FAVORITE THINGS

- Computers
- Scrunchies
- Jelly bracelets

## ICONS OF THE ERA

- Whitney Houston
- Prince
- Michael Jackson

# THE ASPHALT HOODIE
# CROP TOP

This top has that streetwear slickness that's pulled off with ease. It features cap-sleeves, a multi-colored design, and shows the midriff a la Fame in a way that truly embodies the era. I like to wear this with a bodysuit and loose trousers to keep the look seamlessly cool.

## MATERIALS

YARN: Red Heart Super Saver; 100% Acrylic (236 yards/215 meters); medium #4
Neon Stripe: 2 skeins

HOOK: US size 7 (4.5mm) crochet hook

EXTRAS: craft scissors, measuring tape, yarn needle

GAUGE: 11 HDC STS/6 DC ROWS = 4"

## MEASUREMENTS

12+ inches length

## SIZING

SM/MD: [33 inches]

LG/XL: [43 inches]

2XL/3XL: [49 inches]

4XL/5XL: [52 inches]

# THE PATTERN

Begin the hoodie by making two panels. Once the front and back panels are complete, join the pieces at the sides and shoulders. Then add the hood.

Note: Repeat this STEP a total of TWO TIMES for THE FRONT AND BACK PANEL pieces.

## CREATING THE FRONT AND BACK PANEL

### Chain For Total Amount

SM/MD = CH 50 + 3 CHAINS

LG/XL = CH 66 + 3 CHAINS

2XL/3XL = CH 78 + 3 CHAINS

4XL/5XL = CH 82 + 3 CHAINS

**R1:** Insert hook into the 5th CH (the skipped chains count as one DC and CH 1), CH 1, SK 1 ST, *DC in the next ST, CH 1, SK 1 ST; repeat from * until the end of the row. At the end of the row, turn work to continue.

**R2-R16:** CH 3, DC into the first ST, CH 1, SK 1 the CH 1 space, *DC into the next ST, CH 1, SK the CH 1 space; repeat from * until the end of the row. At the end of the row, turn work to continue. At final row, SL ST to complete final work. Do not fasten off.

### Extending Rows

[LG/XL] CONTINUE METHOD UNTIL ROUND 22

[2XL/3XL] CONTINUE METHOD UNTIL ROUND 28

[4XL/5XL] CONTINUE METHOD UNTIL ROUND 32

## CREATING THE SLEEVES

Turn the panel to work horizontally along the side to create the sleeves.

Note: You will repeat this step FOUR times total (TWICE for each side of the crocheted piece).

SM/MD: 15 STS

LG/XL: 18 STS

2XL/3XL: 21 STS

4XL/5XL: 24 STS

**R1-R2:** CH 3, DC into the first ST, CH 1, SK 1 ST, *DC in the next ST, CH 1, SK 1 ST; repeat from * until the end of the row for designated ST amount: [15 (18, 21, 24) STS]. At the end of the row, turn work to continue.

**R3:** CH 2, HDC into 15 (18, 21, 24) STS for the entire row, in between the CH 1 as well. At the end of the row, SL ST to continue work. Fasten off. Weave in ends.

## SEWING THE TOP TOGETHER AT THE SIDE SEAMS

Once both panels are complete, this step is to sew the crocheted panel pieces together to create your top. Lay both pieces flat. Sew the sides together, leaving the armholes open.

## SEWING THE NECKLINE TOGETHER

This step is to sew the shoulders of the top together for the left and right sides. Reinsert your yarn needle and a strand of yarn. Repeat this step TWICE to form the neckline.

### Sew STS For Shoulders:

| | |
|---|---|
| SM/MD: 8 STS | 2XL/3XL: 18 STS |
| LG/XL: 12 STS | 4XL/5XL: 20 STS |

## FORMING THE HOODIE

Working in rows, SL ST to connect. Insert hook into the open neckline working across the BACK PANEL (12 inches length).

**R1:** CH 3, DC into the first ST, CH 1, SK 1 ST, *(DC, CH 1, DC) all into the same open space, CH 1, SK 1 ST; repeat from * until the end of the row. At the end of the row, turn work to continue.

**R2-R7:** CH 3, DC into the first ST, CH 1, SK CH 1 space, *into the next CH space (DC, CH 1, DC) all into same CH space, CH 1; repeat from * until the end of the row. At the end of the row, turn work to continue.

**R8-R14:** CH 3, DC into the first ST, CH 1, SK CH 1 space, *in the CH space (DC, CH 2, DC) all into same CH space, CH 1; repeat from * until the end of the row. At the end of the row, turn work to continue.

At final row, SL ST to complete final work. Do not fasten off.

## SEWING THE HOODIE TOGETHER

Next, you will fold the top of the hoodie together. Turn the rows inside out to sew R14 together.

Use your yarn needle and a strand of yarn to secure the hoodie seam. Fasten off. Weave in ends.

# THE LASER OFF-THE-SHOULDER CROCHET TOP

More fabric means more design! This off-the-shoulder tunic is like a light show with its bright colors and the fit is undeniably cozy. It works well with leather and tight-fitting pants for that clean contrast. It's such a rad garment that when it comes to styling, less is more.

## MATERIALS

YARN: Red Heart Super Saver; 100% Acrylic (236 yards/215 meters); medium #4
Bright Stripe: 3 skeins

HOOK: US size 7 (4.5mm) crochet hook

EXTRAS: craft scissors, measuring tape, yarn needle

GAUGE: 11 HDC STS/6 DC ROWS = 4"

## MEASUREMENTS

22+ inches length

## SIZING

SM/MD: [33 inches]

LG/XL: [43 inches]

2XL/3XL: [49 inches]

4XL/5XL: [52 inches]

# THE PATTERN

The front and back panels are crocheted separately, then sewn together at the side seams and shoulders.

Work from the bottom, up to the armholes, and then to form the shoulders/straps.

**Note:** Repeat this step a total of TWO TIMES for the FRONT AND BACK PANEL pieces.

## CREATING THE FRONT AND BACK PANEL

SM/MD: CH 53 [19 inches]

LG/XL: CH 64 [23 inches]

2XL/3XL: CH 75 [27 inches]

4XL/5XL: CH 86 [31 inches]

**R1:** CH 1, SK 1 CH, SC into all of the STS for the entire row. At the end of the row, turn work to continue.

**R2-R23:** CH 3, DC into all of the STS for the entire row. At the end of the row, turn work to continue.

At final row, SL ST to complete work for this section. Fasten off. Weave in ends.

## EXTENDING SIZING

**R24-R29:** CH 3, DC into all of the STS for the entire row. At the end of the row, turn work to continue.

At final row, SL ST to complete work for this section. Fasten off. Weave in ends.

## CREATING THE ARMHOLES

Skip the first two and last two STS of R23/R29.

Rejoin the hook into the third ST of R23/R29 (after the skipped STS).

SM/MD: 49 STS

LG/XL: 60 STS

2XL/3XL: 71 STS

4XL/5XL: 82 STS

**R24-R29:** CH 3, DC into all the STS for all the rows. At the end of each row, turn work to continue.

### Extending Sizing

**R30-R37:** CH 3, DC into all the STS for all the rows. At the end of each row, turn work to continue. Do not fasten off.

## FORMING THE SHOULDER

For both sides of the top:

### Right Side

SM/MD: 14 STS

LG/XL: 16 STS

2XL/3XL: 18 STS

4XL/5XL: 22 STS

### Left Side

SM/MD: 7 STS

LG/XL: 8 STS

2XL/3XL: 9 STS

4XL/5XL: 11 STS

### RIGHT-SIDE SHOULDER

**R30-R32:** CH 3, DC into all the STS for all the rows. At the end of each row, turn work to continue. [14 (16, 18, 22) STS]

### EXTENDING SIZING

**R38-R39:** CH 3, DC into all of the STS for all of the rows. At the end of each row, turn work to continue.

**R33:** CH 1, SC into all the STS for the entire row, SL ST to complete work for this section. Fasten off. Weave in ends.

**R40:** CH 1, SC into all of the STS for the entire row. At the end of the row, SL ST to complete work for this section. Fasten off. Weave in ends.

### LEFT-SIDE SHOULDER

**R30-R32:** SL ST to rejoin yarn on left side, CH 3, DC into all the STS for all the rows. At the end of each row, turn work to continue. [7 (8, 9, 11) STS]

**R33:** CH 1, SC into all the STS for the entire row, SL ST at the end of the row to complete work for this section. Fasten off. Weave in ends.

### Extending Sizing

**R38-R39:** CH 3, DC into all of the STS for all of the rows. At the end of each row, turn work to continue.

**R40:** CH 1, SC into all of the STS for the entire row. At the end of the row, SL ST to complete work for this section. Fasten off. Weave in ends.

### SEWING THE FRONT AND BACK PANELS TOGETHER

This step is to sew the crocheted panel pieces together to create your top. Once both panels of the top are created, lay both pieces flat. Now, sew the sides together, leaving the armholes, neckline, and the bottom open.

## FORMING THE NECKLINE

This section is to start the NECKLINE by inserting your hook onto the open NECKLINE.

**RND1:** SL ST to join yarn, CH 2, HDC into the first 3 STS, then HDC2TOG for every set of 4 STS to decrease all the STS. At the end of the round, SL ST to continue work.

**RND2-RND3:** CH 2, HDC into all the STS for both rounds. At the end of both rounds, SL ST to continue work.

**RND4:** CH 2, alternate between FPHDC and BPHDC [FPHDC in the next ST, then BPHDC in the next ST] for the entire round. At the end of the round, SL ST to continue work.

**RND5:** CH 1, SC into all the STS for the entire round. At the end of the round, SL ST to complete final work. Fasten off. Weave in ends.

## MAKING THE SLEEVES

**Note:** Repeat this step TWICE.

This section is to start the SLEEVES by inserting your hook onto the open armhole portion for BOTH sides of the top.

SM/MD: DC for 43 STS

LG/XL: DC for 53 STS

2XL/3XL: DC for 57 STS

4XL/5XL: DC for 63 STS

**RND1-RND5:** SL ST to join yarn, CH 3, DC into all the STS for all the rounds [43 (53, 57, 63) STS, SL ST at the end of each round to continue work. Fasten off and weave in ends.

**Note:** Work more rounds before finishing off for personal length desired.

# THE METRO CROCHET SKIRT

This neon skirt makes me feel like I'm riding on the metro. In the 1980s, patterns reigned supreme with electric and neon colors that jump out at you. The white base of the skirt gives the bright colors some balance, allowing you to be more adventurous with your top and shoes. Pair it with denim or a black jacket for that classic flair.

## MATERIALS

YARN: Big Twist Value Worsted Yarns; 100% Acrylic (297 yards/215 meters); medium #4 Bubblegum (Color A), Varsity Gold (Color B), Teal (Color C), Jade Green (Color D), Lilac (Color E), White (Color F): 1 skein each (project used less than half each skein)

HOOK: US size 7 (4.5mm) crochet hook

EXTRAS: craft scissors, measuring tape, yarn needle, sewing needle, matching thread, 2 safety pins, Dritz ½ Braided Elastic 4-½ yard.

WAISTBAND GAUGE: 10 HDC STS = 4"

BOTTOM SKIRT GAUGE: 5 HDC ROWS = 4"

## MEASUREMENTS

13 inches length

## SIZING

SMALL: [25 inches width]

MEDIUM: [33 inches width]

LG/1XL: [41 inches width]

2XL/3XL: [48 inches width]

4XL/5XL: [54 inches width]

# THE PATTERN

The skirt begins with the waistband. The waistband is worked flat, seamed, and the elastic band added. Complete the waistband, then work the skirt in the round from the top down.

## STARTING THE WAISTBAND

Crochet a horizontal piece that will be sewn around the elastic band.

### Sizing

SMALL: 69 STS [25 inches width]

MEDIUM: 95 STS [33 inches width]

LG/1XL: 113 STS [41 inches width]

2XL/3XL: 132 STS [48 inches width]

4XL/5XL: 149 STS [54 inches width]

**R1-R5:** [Color 4] Alternate between SC and HDC into all the STS for ALL the rows [EXAMPLE: R1 = CH 1, SC, R2 = CH 2, HDC], turn work when complete. (Repeat this method until you reach R5.) Once you reach R5, SL ST to complete work. Fasten off. Weave in ends.

## ELASTIC BAND MEASUREMENTS

Cut half an inch longer than waistband measurement to overlap when sewn together.

SMALL: [25.5 inches width]

MEDIUM: [33.5 inches width]

LG//1XL: [41.5 inches width]

2XL/3XL: [48.5 inches width]

4XL/5XL: [54.5 inches width]

## SEW CROCHET WAISTBAND

Folding the crochet piece horizontally in half. Thread the yarn needle with a strand of yarn to sew the folded crochet piece together along the long edge. Leave the sides of the piece open. Cut the yarn and weave in ends.

## INSERT ELASTIC BAND

With the safety pin attached to the elastic, guide the elastic through the crochet waistband. Scrunch to guide the elastic through the crocheted band. Once it is in accordingly, thread your sewing needle with matching thread, overlap the elastic ends for a snug fit, and sew the elastic together.

Make sure it is thread incredibly tight for security. Cut thread and knot.

## BOTTOM OF SKIRT

To start the skirt, work in rounds from the top and to the bottom.

SM: 69 STS [25 inches width]

MD: 93 STS [33 inches width]

LG/1XL: 111 STS [41 inches width]

2XL/3XL: 129 STS [48 inches width]

4XL/5XL: 147 STS [54 inches width]

Long DC – Insert hook into the ST indicated 2 rounds below (this is the ST below the CH), pull up the loop to the height of the STS of the current round to finish the DC ST as normal.

**RND1:** [Color F] CH 2, HDC in around the waistband for 69 (95, 113, 132, 149) STS, SL ST at the end of the round to join and continue work.

**RND2:** [Color F] CH 3 (counts as a DC), DC in next 2 STS, *CH 3, SK 3 STS, DC in next 3 STS; repeat from * around, SL ST at the end of the round to join and continue work.

**RND3:** [Color A] CH 3, SK the first 3 DC STS, *Long DC in the ST two rounds below (THREE TIMES), CH 3, SK the next 3 DC; repeat from * around, SL ST at the end of the round to join and continue work.

**RND4:** [Color F] CH 3 (counts as the first DC), Long DC in the ST two rounds below (TWO TIMES), *CH 3, SK the first 3 DC, Long DC in the ST two rounds below (THREE TIMES); repeat from * around, SL ST at the end of the round to join and continue work.

**RND5-RND28:** Follow the color sequence below for each round. Alternate between working RND3 and RND4 for ALL the rounds [RND5 = work same as RND3, RND6 = work same as RND4, RND7 = work same as RND3, RND8 = work same as RND4]. Join with a SL ST at the end of every round. Once you've completed RND27, join with SL ST. Do not fasten off.

**RND5:** [Color E]

**RND6:** [Color F]

**RND7:** [Color C]

**RND8:** [Color F]

**RND9:** [Color D]

**RND10:** [Color F]

**RND11:** [Color B]

**RND12:** [Color F]

**RND13:** [Color A]

**RND14:** [Color F]

**RND15:** [Color E]

**RND16:** [Color F]

**RND17:** [Color C]

**RND18:** [Color F]

**RND19:** [Color A]

**RND20:** [Color F]

**RND21:** [Color E]

**RND22:** [Color F]

**RND23:** [Color C]

**RND24:** [Color F]

**RND25:** [Color D]

**RND26:** [Color F]

**RND27:** [Color B]

**Note:** For personal desired length, continue adding rounds, alternating colors following sequence to desired length.

**RND28:** [Color F] CH 1, SC around and into all the STS for the entire round, then connect by SL ST to complete final work. Fasten off. Weave in ends.

# THE NEON DREAM CROCHET CARDIGAN

The '80s were a time of flash and color. In the vein of *Joseph and the Amazing Technicolor Dreamcoat*, this half-sleeved drop cardigan bedazzles with a multi-colored pattern that catches the eye immediately. It's where fashion meets spectacle!

## MATERIALS

YARN: Red Heart Super Saver; 100% Acrylic (236 yards/215 meters); medium #4
Black Light: 3 skeins

HOOK: US size 7 (4.5mm) crochet hook

EXTRAS: craft scissors, measuring tape, yarn needle

GAUGE: 12 HDC STS/6 DC ROWS = 4"

## MEASUREMENTS

13.5 inches length

## SIZING

SM/MD: [29 inches width]

LG/XL: [43 inches width]

2XL/3XL: [50 inches width]

4XL/5XL: [54 inches width]

# THE PATTERN

The front and back panels are worked separately. Working from the bottom up and then to form the sleeves.

## CREATING THE BACK PANEL

SM/MD: CH 42 [15.25 inches width]

LG/XL: CH 63 [23 inches width]

2XL/3XL: CH 75 [27.25 inches width]

4XL/5XL: CH 81 [29.5 inches width]

**R1:** CH 2, SK 2 CH, HDC across into all the STS for the entire row. At end of row, turn work to continue.

**R2-R12:** CH 3, DC across into all the STS for each row. At end of each row, turn work to continue.

At final row [R12], SL ST to complete work for this section. Fasten off. Weave in ends.

### Extended Lengths

**R13-R18:** CH 3, DC across into all the STS for each row. At end of each row, turn work to continue.

At final row [R18], SL ST to complete work for this section. Fasten off. Weave in ends.

## CREATING ARMHOLES

Skip the first two and last two STS of R12/18.

Reinsert hook into the 3rd ST of R12/18 (after the skipped STS).

SM/MD: 38 STS

LG/XL: 59 STS

2XL/3XL: 71 STS

4XL/5XL: 77 STS

**R13-R18:** CH 3, DC across into all the 38 (59, 71, 77) STS for each row. At the end of each row, turn work to continue.

### Extended Lengths

**R19-R26:** CH 3, DC across into all the STS for each row. At end of each row, turn work to continue.

## FORMING THE SHOULDER

### First Shoulder

SM/MD: 12 STS

LG/XL: 14 STS

2XL/3XL: 16 STS

4XL/5XL: 16 STS

**R19:** CH 3, DC across into all the 12 (14, 16, 16) STS for each row. At end of each row, turn work to continue. Leave remaining STS unworked.

**R20:** CH 1, SC across into all the STS for the entire row, SL ST at end of row to complete work for this section. Fasten off. Weave in ends.

### Extended Lengths

**R27:** CH 3, DC across into all the STS for each row. At the end of each row, turn work to continue.

**R28:** CH 1, SC across into all the STS for the entire row, SL ST at end of row to complete work for this section. Fasten off. Weave in ends.

### Second Shoulder

Rejoin yarn with SL ST to the other end, work the same as FIRST SHOULDER, starting with R19/R27. Fasten off. Weave in ends.

## CREATING THE FRONT RIGHT-SIDE PANEL

Working from the bottom, then to form the shoulder.

SM/MD: CH 21 [7.5 inches width]

LG/XL: CH 31 [11.25 inches width]

2XL/3XL: CH 37 [13.5 inches width]

4XL/5XL: CH 40 [14.5 inches width]

**R1:** CH 2, SK 2 CH, HDC across into all the STS for the entire row. At end of row, turn work to continue.

**R2-R12:** CH 3, DC across into all the STS for each row. At end of each row, turn work to continue.

At final row [R12], SL ST to complete work for this section. Fasten off. Weave in ends.

### Extended Lengths

**R13-R18:** CH 3, DC across into all the STS for each row. At the end of each row, turn work to continue.

At final row [R18], SL ST to complete work for this section. Fasten off. Weave in ends.

## CREATING THE ARMHOLES

Skip the first two STS of armhole end of R12/18.

Reinsert hook into the 3rd ST of R12/18 (after the skipped STS).

SM/MD: 19 STS

LG/XL: 29 STS

2XL/3XL: 35 STS

4XL/5XL: 38 STS

**R13-R18:** CH 3, DC across into all the 19 (29, 35, 38) STS for each row. At end of each row, turn work to continue.

### Extended Lengths

**R19-R26:** CH 3, DC across into all the 19 (29, 35, 38) STS for each row. At end of each row, turn work to continue.

## SHOULDERS FOR THE RIGHT SIDE

SM/MD: 8 STS

LG/XL: 14 STS

2XL/3XL: 17 STS

4XL/5XL: 17 STS

**R19:** CH 3, DC across into all the 8 (14, 17, 17) STS for each row. At the end of each row, turn work to continue, leaving the remaining STS unworked.

**R20:** CH 1, SC across into all the STS for the entire row. At the end of row, SL ST to complete work for this section. Fasten off. Weave in ends.

### Extended Lengths

**R27:** CH 3, DC across into all of the STS for each row. At the end of each row, turn work to continue.

**R28:** CH 1, SC across into all of the STS for the entire row. At the end of row, SL ST to complete work for this section. Fasten off. Weave in ends.

## CREATING THE FRONT LEFT-SIDE PANEL

Work from the bottom then to form the shoulders.

SM/MD: CH 21 [7.5 inches width]

LG/XL: CH 31 [11.25 inches width]

2XL/3XL: CH 37 [13.5 inches width]

4XL/5XL: CH 40 [14.5 inches width]

**R1:** CH 2, SK 2, HDC across into all the STS for the entire row. At the end of row, turn work to continue.

**R2-R12:** CH 3, DC across into all the STS for each row. At the end of each row, turn work to continue.

At final row [R12], SL ST to complete work for this section.

### Extended Lengths

**R2-R18:** DC across into all the STS for each row. At the end of each row, turn work to continue.

At final row [R18], SL ST to complete work for this section.

## CREATING THE ARMHOLES

Skip the first two STS of R12/18.

Reinsert hook into the 3rd ST of R12/18 (after the skipped STS).

SM/MD: 19 STS

LG/XL: 29 STS

2XL/3XL: 35 STS

4XL/5XL: 38 STS

**R13-R18:** CH 3, DC across into all the 19 (29, 35, 38) STS for each row. At the end of each row, turn work to continue.

### Extended Lengths

**R19-R26:** CH 3, DC across into all the 19 (29, 35, 38) STS for each row. At end of each row, turn work to continue.

### Create Left Shoulder

Block your completed pieces (OPTIONAL).

You will lay both pieces flat and thoroughly wet the pieces (with a spray bottle). Lay the piece flat and gently create the shape into the desired finished measurements.

## SEWING CARDIGAN

This step is to sew the BACK PANEL, FRONT RIGHT-SIDE PANEL, and FRONT LEFT SIDE PANELS together to create your cardigan. Lay ALL pieces flat. Now sew the sides together, leaving the armholes, neckline, and the bottom of the top free once the sewing is complete.

## CREATING THE SLEEVES

To create the sleeves, work in rounds joined with SL ST. Insert hook into the OPEN armhole at the underarm. We will repeat for BOTH sides. (12 inches in length or to desired length). Rejoin yarn into the open armhole space created for both LEFT and RIGHT sides, respectively.

SM/MD: 35 STS

LG/1XL: 43 STS

2XL/3XL: 47 STS

4XL/5XL: 54 STS

**RND1:** Join with SL ST, CH 2, HDC into all the 35 (43, 47, 54) STS for the entire round. At the end of the round, SL ST to continue work.

**RND2-RND16:** CH 3, DC into all the STS for each round. At the end of the each, SL ST to continue work.

At final desired round, SL ST to complete final work. Fasten off. Weave in ends.

**Note:** Extend rounds within this section for desired personal length.

## FINISHING TECHNIQUE

Join yarn with SL ST at front-left bottom edge, CH 1, SC once around the entire crocheted cardigan. Fasten off. Weave in ends.

# THE RAD CROCHET CLUTCH

This bag is chaos incarnate. I think there's beauty in randomness and this bag captures that feeling with splashes of paint color as the design.

## MATERIALS

**YARN:** Big Twist Value Worsted Yarns; 100% Acrylic (297 yards/215 meters); medium #4 Coral (Color A), Sapphire (Color B): 1 skein each (project used less than half each skein) Red Heart Super Saver; 100% Acrylic (364 yards/198 meters); medium #4 Spring Green (Color C), Bright Yellow (Color D), White (Color E): 1 skein each (project used less than half each skein)

**HOOK:** US size 7 (4.5mm) crochet hook

**EXTRAS:** craft scissors, measuring tape, yarn needle, sewing needle, matching thread, [1] 9 × 12 fabric fat square, fabric adhesive or glue gun, [1] 13-inch metal zipper

**GAUGE:** 11 HDC STS/9 HDC ROWS = 4"

## MEASUREMENTS

8.25 inches length × 14.5 inches width

# THE PATTERN

The clutch is worked in two pieces. The front panel has a graphic and back is plain.

## CREATING THE FRONT PANEL

CH 35.

**R1:** [Color E] CH 2, HDC into all the STS for the entire row. At the end of the row, turn work to continue. [35 STS TOTAL]

**FROM LEFT SIDE: R2:** [Color A] HDC 8 STS---[Color E] HDC 5 STS---[Color C] HDC 14 STS---[Color E] HDC 4 STS---[Color D] HDC 4 STS. At the end of the row, turn work to continue.

**RIGHT SIDE: R3:** [Color D] HDC 4 STS---[Color E] HDC 5 STS---[Color C] HDC 12 STS---[Color E] HDC 7 STS---[Color A] HDC 6 STS---[Color E] HDC 1 ST. At the end of the row, turn work to continue.

**LEFT SIDE: R4:** [Color E] HDC 2 STS---[Color A] HDC 4 STS---[Color E] HDC 3 STS---[Color A] HDC 2 STS---[Color E] HDC 4 STS---[Color C] HDC 9 STS---[Color E] HDC 3 STS---[Color C] HDC 1 ST---[Color E] HDC 3 STS---[Color D] HDC 4 STS. At the end of the row, turn work to continue.

**RIGHT SIDE: R5:** [Color D] HDC 3 STS---[Color E] HDC 4 ST---[Color C] HDC 1 ST---[Color E] HDC 5 STS---[Color C] HDC 6 STS---[Color E] HDC 5 STS---[Color A] HDC 2 STS---[Color E] HDC 2 STS---[Color A] HDC 5 STS---[Color E] HDC 2 ST. At the end of the row, turn work to continue.

**LEFT SIDE: R6:** [Color E] HDC 2 STS---[Color A] HDC 5 STS---[Color E] HDC 6 STS---[Color C] HDC 1 ST---[Color E] HDC 2 STS---[Color C] HDC 6 STS---[Color E] HDC 2 STS---[Color D] HDC 2 STS---[Color E] HDC 6 STS---[Color D] HDC 3 STS. At the end of the row, turn work to continue.

**RIGHT SIDE: R7:** [Color D] HDC 3 STS---[Color E] HDC 6 STS---[Color D] HDC 2 STS---[Color E] HDC 2 STS---[Color C] HDC 4 STS---[Color E] HDC 1 ST---[Color C] HDC 3 STS---[Color E] HDC 5 STS---[Color A] HDC 3 STS---[Color E] HDC 2 STS---[Color A] HDC 4 STS. At the end of the row, turn work to continue.

**LEFT SIDE: R8:** [Color A] HDC 2 STS---[Color E] HDC 3 STS---[Color A] HDC 4 STS---[Color E] HDC 3 STS---[Color A] HDC 2 STS---[Color E] HDC 1 ST---[Color C ] HDC 3 STS---[Color E] HDC 3 STS---[Color C] HDC 2 STS---[Color E] HDC 4 STS---[Color C] HDC 2 STS---[Color E] HDC 1 ST---[Color D] HDC 5 STS. At the end of the row, turn work to continue.

**RIGHT SIDE: R9:** [Color D] HDC 5 STS---[Color E] HDC 13 STS---[Color C] HDC 1 ST---[Color E] HDC 7 STS---[Color A] HDC 2 STS---[Color E] HDC 4 STS---[Color A] HDC 3 STS. At the end of the row, turn work to continue.

**LEFT SIDE: R10:** [Color A] HDC 2 STS---[Color E] HDC 3 STS---[Color A] HDC 1 ST---[Color E] HDC 4 STS---[Color B] HDC 2 STS---[Color E] HDC 6 STS---[Color C] HDC 3 STS---[Color E] HDC 5 STS---[Color D] HDC 1 ST -[Color E] HDC 2 STS---[Color D] HDC 6 STS. At the end of the row, turn work to continue.

**RIGHT SIDE: R11:** [Color D] HDC 6 STS---[Color E] HDC 2 STS---[Color D] HDC 1 ST---[Color E] HDC 5 STS---[Color C] HDC 3 STS---[Color E] HDC 3 STS---[Color B] HDC 1 ST---[Color E] HDC 8 STS---[Color A] HDC 1 ST---[Color E] HDC 5 STS. At the end of the row, turn work to continue.

**LEFT SIDE: R12:** [Color E] HDC 2 STS---[Color B] HDC 1 ST---[Color E] HDC 5 STS---[Color B] HDC 3 STS---[Color E] HDC 2 STS---[Color B] HDC 3 STS---[Color E] HDC 6 STS---[Color C] HDC 1 ST---[Color E] HDC 5 STS---[Color D] HDC 7 STS. At the end of the row, turn work to continue.

**RIGHT SIDE: R13:** [Color D] HDC 10 STS---[Color E] HDC 5 STS---[Color D] HDC 2 STS---[Color E] HDC 2 STS---[Color B] HDC 9 STS---[Color E] HDC 1 ST---[Color A] HDC 2 STS---[Color E] HDC 4 STS. At the end of the row, turn work to continue.

## CREATING THE BACK PANEL

CH 35.

**R1-R17:** [Color E] CH 2, HDC into all the STS for all the rows. At the end of each row, turn work to continue

**LEFT SIDE: R14:** [Color E] HDC 7 STS---[Color B] HDC 10 STS---[Color E] HDC 6 STS---[Color D] HDC 12 STS. At the end of the row, turn work to continue.

**RIGHT SIDE: R15:** [Color D] HDC 12 STS---[Color E] HDC 1 ST---(Color B] HDC 2 STS---[Color E] HDC 4 STS---[Color B] HDC 10 STS---[Color E] HDC 5 STS---[Color B] HDC 1 ST. At the end of the row, turn work to continue.

**LEFT SIDE: R16:** [Color B] HDC 1 ST---[Color E] HDC 5 STS--(Color B] HDC 10 STS---[Color E] HDC 4 STS---[Color B] HDC 2 STS---[Color D] HDC 13 STS. At the end of the row, turn work to continue.

**RIGHT SIDE: R17:** [Color D] HDC 13 STS---[Color E] HDC 3 STS--(Color D] HDC 1 ST---[Color E] HDC 3 STS---[Color B] HDC 10 STS---[Color E] HDC 1 ST---[Color A] HDC 1 ST --[Color E] HDC 3 STS. At the end of the row, turn work to continue.

**R18:** [Color E] SC into all the STS for the entire row, SL ST at the end of the row to complete work for this section. Fasten off. Weave in ends.

**R18:** [Color E] CH 1, SC into all the STS for the entire row. At the end of the row, SL ST at the end of the row to complete work for this section. Fasten off. Weave in ends.

## ADDING THE FABRIC LINING

Cut off 2 SETS of fabric from the fat square. Cut around the finished crochet FRONT AND BACK PANEL pieces a little less than 12.5 inches length × 8 inches width. Sew or utilize fabric glue adhesive to apply the fabric to the back of the finished crochet pieces

## IMPLEMENTING THE ZIPPER

Lay both FRONT and BACK panels horizontally to sew [R16]. Secure both crocheted panels sides to each side of the zipper lining sides.

## SEWING THE BAG TOGETHER

With a yarn needle and a strand of yarn, sew the sides and the bottom of the bag [FRONT and BACK]. Weave in any remaining ends.

# RADICAL SHAPES CROCHET BAG

Have fun with shapes and colors with this geometric 80's-inspired crochet bag. Experiment with fun and bold colors that proudly represent the adoration of all things abstract and vibrant!

## MATERIALS

YARN: Big Twist Value Worsted Yarns; 100% Acrylic (297 yards/215 meters); medium #4 Varsity Red (Color A), Varsity Green (Color B), Varsity Orange (Color C)
Red Heart Super Saver; 100% Acrylic (364 yards/198 meters); medium #4
Saffron (Color D), Royal (Color E): 1 skein each (project used less than half each skein)

HOOK: US size 7 (4.5mm) crochet hook

EXTRAS: 2 [9 × 12] felt squares or 2 Fabric Fat Squares (Red), craft scissors, measuring tape, fabric glue or hot glue gun, needle and thread, fabric pen, yarn needle, 1 purse strap, 2 metal jump rings, jewelry pliers (to open the jump rings)

GAUGE: 12 HDC STS/9 HDC ROWS= 4"

## BAG SIZE MEASUREMENT

8.5 inches length × 10 inches width

# THE PATTERN

## CREATING THE FRONT OF THE BAG • • • • • • • • • • • • • • • • • • • • • • • •

Constructing four separate squares to attach and create the front of the bag.

### Square 1

[Color A] CH FOR 13.

**R1:** CH 1, SC across into all the STS for the entire row. At end of row, turn work to continue.

**R2-R8:** CH 2, HDC across into all the STS for each row. At end of each row, turn work to continue.

**R9:** CH 1, SC across into all the STS for the entire row. At end of row, SL ST to complete work for this section. Fasten off. Weave in ends.

### Square 2

[Color B] CH FOR 13 STS

**R1:** CH 1, SC across into all the STS for the entire row. At end of row, turn work to continue.

**R2-R8:** CH 2, HDC across into all the STS for each row. At end of each row, turn work to continue.

**R9:** CH 1, SC across into all the STS for the entire row. At end of row, SL ST to complete work for this section. Fasten off. Weave in ends.

## Square 3

[Color D] CH FOR 13.

**R1:** CH 1, SC across into all the STS for the entire row. At end of row, turn work to continue.

**R2-R8:** CH 2, HDC across into all the STS for each row. At end of each row, turn work to continue.

**R9:** CH 1, SC across into all the STS for the entire row. At end of row, SL ST to complete work for this section. Fasten off. Weave in ends.

## Square 4

[Color E] CH FOR 13.

**R1:** CH 1, SK the first CH, SC across into all the CH for the entire row. At end of row, turn work to continue.

**R2-R8:** CH 2, HDC across into all the STS for each row. At end of each row, turn work to continue.

**R9:** CH 1, SC across into all the STS for the entire row. At end of row, SL ST to complete work for this section. Fasten off. Weave in ends.

## SEWING THE 4 SQUARES OF FRONT PANELS TOGETHER

Next, utilizing your yarn sewing needle and 2 sets of a long strand of yarn, sew both vertical and horizontally, all 4 squares together, to create one large square. Combining all of the individual squares as one FRONT panel.

## CREATING THE BACK OF THE BAG

[Color C] CH FOR 26.

**R1:** CH 1, SC across into all the STS for the entire row. At end of row, turn work to continue.

**R2-R17:** CH 2, HDC across into all the STS for each row. At end of each row, turn work to continue.

**R18:** CH 1, SC across into all the STS for the entire row. At end of row, SL ST to complete work for this section. Fasten off. Weave in ends.

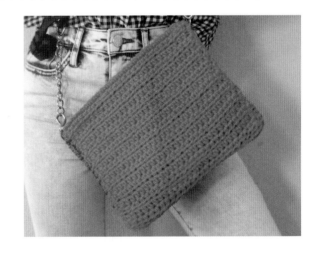

## SEWING THE BACK AND FRONT PANELS TOGETHER

Next, utilizing your yarn sewing needle and 3 sets of a long strand of yarn, sew both vertical sides and the bottom horizontal of the bag, FRONT AND BACK together, leaving the top open.

## ATTACHING THE FABRIC LINING

Turn the bag inside out. Cut 2 SETS of fabric from the fat square or felt square, cutting around the finished crochet FRONT AND BACK PANEL pieces a little less than [8.5 inches length × 10 inches width] to either sew or utilize fabric glue adhesive, to apply to the back of the finished crochet pieces to secure it in place.

## ATTACHING THE METAL JUMP RINGS

Using the jewelry pliers, open the metal jump ring, guide the jump ring through the top side corner of the bag.  Repeat for the other side of the bag.

## ATTACHING THE PURSE STRAP

Opening the clasp, guide the purse strap through the metal jump ring, enclosing both rings for each side.

# THE 1990s

The '90s are my era. I have so many firsthand memories that are still fresh in my mind, from using AOL to collecting slap bracelets. I loved reading, and *The Baby-Sitters Club* books were my favorite. I never missed an episode of *Full House,* and I watched an intense amount of cartoons. As for music, nothing beats '90s R&B. There were so many good jams that still sound amazing today. I was deeply invested in the war of the boy bands and watched as my friends argued about Christina Aguilera vs. Britney Spears; there was always something exciting going on. This decade is unforgettable, which is why '90s trends return so frequently. It is hard to beat the era that gave us the Spice Girls AND the Nintendo 64.

## FAVORITE MOVIES

- *Titanic*
- *Edward Scissorhands*
- *The Fifth Element*

## FAVORITE TV SHOWS

- *Full House*
- *All That*
- *Even Stevens*

## OTHER FAVORITE THINGS

- *Tamagotchi*
- *Furby*
- *Mario Kart 64*

## ICONS OF THE ERA

- *Aaliyah*
- *Christina Aguilera*
- *Halle Berry*

# THE TOTALLY BUGGIN' CROCHET MINI BACKPACK

Flower power was alive and well even in the '90s. This double-strapped backpack has three daisy patterns on the flap for that romantic detail. It's perfect for school and all your crafty creations. It fits books, writing utensils, yarn, scissors, and more yarn.

## MATERIALS

YARN: Mainstays; 100% Acrylic (251 yards/230 meters); medium #4 Sweet Violet: 1 skein each

HOOK: US size 7 (4.5mm) crochet hook

EXTRAS: [1 yard] fat fabric square (purple), craft scissors, measuring tape, fabric glue or hot glue gun, fabric pen, yarn needle, sewing needle, matching thread, 3 daisy flower appliques, 1 set of nylon strapping 1 × 60 inch in purple (2.54cm × 1.52cm), 1 set of sew-on snaps size 10, 21mm

GAUGE: 10 HDC STS/11 HDC ROWS = 4"

## MEASUREMENTS

22 inches width × 9 inches length

# THE PATTERN

The bag begins with the base worked in the round. Once the base is complete, continue to work up the sides without increasing. The flap is worked flat. The strap is sewn on.

### CREATING THE BASE OF THE BAG

CH 18.

**RND1:** SK 1 CH, HDC into each 16 STS, 6 HDC into the last ST, continue working on the other side, HDC into each of the 16 STS until you reach the last ST, work 6 HDC into the beginning ST, join with SL ST to the first HDC ST.

**RND2:** CH 2 (does not counted as a ST), HDC into same ST, HDC into all the STS until you reach the 6 HDC, then 2 HDC into each of the 6 HDC. Next, working on the other side, HDC into each of the STS until you reach the 6 HDC, work 2 HDC into each of the STS, join with SL ST to the first HDC.

**RND3:** CH 2 (does not counted as a ST), HDC into same ST, HDC into all the STS until you reach the corner, (note: the first set of the 2 HDC), *HDC into the next 2 STS, 2 HDC into following ST; repeat from * into the 6 HDC set until you reach the corner.

Working the other side, HDC into all of the STS until you reach the corner, *HDC into the next 2 HDC, 2 HDC in the following ST; repeat from * into the 6 HDC set, join with SL ST to the first DC.

### CREATING THE BODY OF THE BAG

**RND4-RND19:** CH 2, HDC into the STS made from the previous round, for all the rounds. At the end of each round, SL ST to continue work. At the final round [RND19], SL ST to complete final work. Fasten off. Weave in ends.

### CREATING THE FLAP OF THE BAG

**R1:** Reinsert your hook into the BACK of the bag and join with a SL ST, CH 2, HDC in between the STS for 19 STS, creating the first row, turn to continue work.

**R2-R8:** CH 2, HDC in between the STS made from the previous row for all the rows, SL ST at the end of each row to continue work.

**R9:** CH 1, SC into all the STS, for the entire row [19 STS], SL ST at the end of the row to complete final work. Fasten off. Weave in ends.

## ADDING THE FABRIC

Cut a few centimeters short of 8 wide × 3.5 length inches for the flap of the bag.

Cut a few centimeters short of 23 wide × 8 length inches for the inside of the bag.

Turn the bag inside out. Use the fabric glue adhesive, sewing needle and matching thread, or a hot glue gun and apply the fabric from the fat square to the inside and flap of the bag.

## CREATING THE STRAPS

Cut a 28 inches width from the nylon straps TWICE.

Sew the straps to the back top of the bag [at RND18] and the back bottom of the bag [at RND3] 7 inches apart. Weave in any remaining ends.

## ADDING THE FLORAL APPLIQUE

Using fabric adhesive or hot glue gun, apply glue to the back of the appliques. Set one applique on the flap of the bag as well as two appliques [3 inches apart] to the FRONT BODY of the bag.

You may place the floral appliques however personally desired!

Using a sewing needle and matching thread, sew the edges of the applique through the crocheted body of the bag and through the applique, securing the detail onto the bag.

## TUCKING THE BAG

Using a yarn needle and a strand of yarn, at the top of the bag, fold the top sides of the bag towards the inside, pinching the ends. Insert the yarn needle through the side of the crochet fold together. Secure the cinched appearance for the bag.

**Note:** Repeat method for the opposite top side of the bag.

## INSERTING SEW-ON SNAPS

Add the snap to the center of the flap, starting with the socket side. Using sewing needle and thread, sew through the opening of the snaps, securing it to the inside fabric for the flap.

Match the location of the closure of the sew-on snap (from the flap to the base).

Noting where it closes, sew with needle and thread, the opposite snap (the ball socket), securing it to the body of the bag.

# THE BLING TRIO CROCHET CHOKERS

Who says chokers must be so hard-edged? These chokers take a softer approach with a lighter pallet and cloud charms, making this an inviting aesthetic. The silver jeweled buckle detail and pearls offer a touch of class to this daring remix.

## MATERIALS

**Note:** Be sure to experiment with different charms and accessories for your chokers!

YARN: Caron Simply Soft Yarn; 100% Acrylic (364 yards/288 meters); medium #4 Orchid (Color A), Soft Blue (Color B), Pink (Color C): 1 skein each (project used less than half each skein)

HOOK: US size 7 (4.5mm) crochet hook

EXTRAS: (6) 10mm metal jump rings, 5 cloud charms, 1 pearl charm "Hildie & Jo" ornamented silver & gold charm pack, (1) 15mm rhinestone buckle slider, craft scissors, measuring tape, pliers (to open the jump rings), yarn needle

GAUGE: 11 CHS = 4"

## MEASUREMENTS

8 inches length

# THE PATTERNS

Each choker is made from basic chain stitches and embellished. The length is easily adjustable by making more or fewer chains.

## THE CLOUD CHARM CHOKER

CH 21 [Color B].

**R1:** CH 3, SK 3 CH, DC into the next CH, *CH 1, SK 1 CH, DC into the next CH; repeat from * until the end of the row, ending on a single DC ST, SL ST to complete final work. Fasten off. Weave in ends.

### Creating the Straps for the Choker

**Note:** Repeat this step TWICE, once FOR BOTH SIDES.

Reinsert hook into the side open space of the row, join yarn with SL ST, CH for 14 STS. Fasten off. Weave in ends.

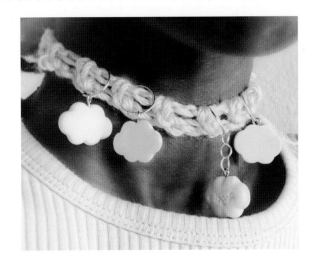

### Adding the Charms

To add charm to the metal jump rings, use the pliers to open both clasps to insert and guide the jump rings through the open chained crochet spaces created from R1.

**Note:** Add as many charms or as little as you desire!

## THE RHINESTONE SLIDER CHOKE

CH 24 [Color A].

**R1-R2:** CH 2, SK 2 CH, HDC into all the STS. For both rows, turn work at the end of the row to continue. SL ST at the end of the final row to complete work. Fasten off. Weave in ends.

### Adding the Slider

Slide the buckle through the completed crocheted piece until it lands in the middle of the finished choker.

Creating the Straps for the Choker

Note: Repeat this step TWICE, once FOR BOTH SIDES.

Reinsert hook into the side open space of the row, join yarn with SL ST, CH for 14 STS. Fasten off. Weave in ends.

### THE PEARL SLIDER CHOKER

CH 24 [Color C].

**R1:** CH 1, SK 1 CH, SC into all of the STS for the entire row. At the end of the row, turn work to continue.

**R2:** CH 3 (counts as first DC), *SK 1 ST, DC into the next ST, return to the skipped ST and DC into that skipped ST (the STS form an X); repeat from * until 1 ST remains at the end of row, DC into the last ST, turn work.

**R3:** CH 1, SC into all the STS for the entire row. SL ST at the end of the row to complete final work. Fasten off. Weave in ends.

### ADDING THE PEARL

Add the pearl charm to the metal jump rings. Open the clasp to insert the jump ring into the middle ST created from R1.

### CREATING THE STRAPS

Note: Repeat this step TWICE, once FOR BOTH SIDES [LEFT & RIGHT SIDES RESPECTIVELY]

Reinsert hook into the side and into the middle ST between the two rows, join yarn with SL ST, CH for 14 STS. Fasten off. Weave in ends.

# BUTTERFLY STRIPED CROCHET VEST TOP

Some items feel like pure bliss and that can be said for this cozy sweater vest! This four-colored striped top is subtly dynamic in its classic presentation, with a dreamy design that works well when you're in a whimsical mood. Pairing it with your favorite blouse can take your outfit to a completely new world.

## MATERIALS

YARN: Red Heart Super Saver; 100% Acrylic (364 yards/198 meters); medium #4 Orchid (Color A), Baby Blue (Color B), Bright Yellow (Color C), Pretty in Pink (Color D), Minty (Color E): 1 skein each (project used less than half each skein)

HOOK: US size 7 (4.5mm) crochet hook

EXTRAS: 1 Butterfly applique (2 inches), sewing needle, matching thread, craft scissors, measuring tape, fabric glue or hot glue gun, yarn needle

GAUGE: 11 HDC STS/9 HDC ROWS = 4"

## MEASUREMENTS

12.5 inches

## SIZING

SM/MD: [33 inches]

LG/XL: [43 inches]

2XL/3XL: [49 inches]

4XL/5XL: [52 inches]

# THE PATTERN

The vest is worked in panels [front and back]. Working from the waist to the bust/back, then onto creating the shoulders.

**Note:** You will repeat this STEP a total of TWO TIMES for THE FRONT AND BACK PANEL pieces.

## CREATING THE FRONT AND BACK PANEL

SM/MD: CH for 53 STS [19 inches]

LG/XL: CH for 64 STS [23 inches]

2XL/3XL: CH for 75 STS [27 inches]

4XL/5XL: CH for 86 STS [31 inches]

**R1:** [Color E] CH 1, SC into all the 53 (64, 75, 86) STS for the entire row. At the end of the row, turn work to continue.

**R2-R3:** [Color E] CH 2, HDC into all of the STS for the entire row. At the end of the row, turn work to continue.

**R4-R6:** [Color C] CH 2, HDC into all of the STS for the entire row. At the end of the row, turn work to continue.

**R7:** [Color A] CH 2, HDC into all of the STS for the entire row. At the end of the row, turn work to continue.

**R8-R10:** [Color B] CH 2, HDC into all of the STS for the entire row. At the end of the row, turn work to continue.

**R11-R13:** [Color D] CH 2, HDC into all of the STS for the entire row. At the end of the row, turn work to continue.

**R14:** [Color A] CH 2, HDC into all of the STS for the entire row, SL ST at the end of the row to complete work for this section. Fasten off. Weave in ends.

### Extended Lengths

**R15-R17:** [Color E] CH 2, HDC into all of the 53 (64, 75, 86) for the entire row. At the end of the row, turn work to continue.

**R18-20:** [Color C] CH 2, HDC into all of the STS for the entire row. At the end of the row, turn work to continue.

**R21:** [Color A] CH 2, HDC into all of the STS for the entire row. SL ST at the end of the row to complete work for this section. Fasten off. Weave in ends.

## CREATING THE ARMHOLE

Skip the first two and last two STS of R14/R21.

Reinsert hook into the 3rd ST of R14/R21 (after the skipped STS).

SM/MD: 49 STS

LG/XL: 60 STS

2XL/3XL: 71 STS

4XL/5XL: 82 STS

**R15-R17:** [Color E] CH 2, HDC into all the 49 (60, 71, 82) STS for the entire row. At the end of the row, turn work to continue.

**R18-R20:** [Color C] CH 2, HDC into all the STS for the entire row. At the end of the row, turn work to continue.

**R21:** [Color A] CH 2, HDC into all the STS for the entire row. At the end of the row, turn work to continue.

**R22-R24:** [Color B] CH 2, HDC into all the STS for the entire row. At the end of the row, turn work to continue.

**R25-R27:** [Color D] CH 2, HDC into all the STS for the entire row. At the end of the row, turn work to continue.

### Extending Sizing

**R22-R24:** [Color B] CH 2, HDC into all of the 49 (60, 71, 82) STS for the entire row. At the end of the row, turn work to continue.

**R25-R27:** [Color D] CH 2, HDC into all of the STS for the entire row. At the end of the row, turn work to continue.

**R28:** [Color A] CH 2, HDC into all of the STS for the entire row. At the end of the row, turn work to continue.

**R29-R31:** [Color E] CH 2, HDC into all of the STS for the entire row. At the end of the row, turn work to continue.

**R32-R34:** [Color C] CH 2, HDC into all of the STS for the entire row. At the end of the row, turn work to continue.

## FORMING THE SHOULDER

Repeat this step for BOTH sides (left and right) for the same row.

SM/MD: 14 STS

LG/XL: 16 STS

2XL/3XL: 18 STS

4XL/5XL: 22 STS

**R28:** [Color D] CH 1, SC into all the shoulder 14 (16, 18, 22) STS for the entire row. At the end of the row, SL ST to complete work for this section. Fasten off. Weave in ends.

### Extending Sizing

**R35:** [Color A] CH 1, SC into all the shoulder 14 (16, 18, 22) STS for the entire row. At the end of the row, SL ST to complete work for this section. Fasten off. Weave in ends.

**R36:** [Color D] Join yarn with SL ST, CH 1, SC into all the shoulder 14 (16, 18, 22) STS for the entire row. At the end of the row, SL ST to complete work for this section. Fasten off. Weave in ends.

## SEWING THE FRONT AND BACK PANELS TOGETHER

This step is to sew the crocheted pieces together to create your top. Once both parts of the top are created, lay both pieces flat. Sew the sides together, leaving the armholes, neckline, and the bottom of the top free.

## FINISHING TECHNIQUE NECKLINE

This section is to start the NECKLINE of the TOP by inserting your hook into the side ST of the open Neckline.

**RND1:** [Color B] Join yarn with SL ST at left shoulder, CH 1, SC into all the STS for all the round. SL ST at the end of the round to complete final work. Fasten off. Weave in ends.

## CREATING THE SLEEVES

Note: Repeat this step TWICE, once for each sleeve.

Start the sleeves by inserting your hook into the open armhole portion, for BOTH sides of the top.

SM/MD: 43 STS

LG/XL: 53 STS

2XL-5XL: 63 STS

**RND1:** [Color B] Join yarn with SL ST, CH 1, SC into all the STS for all the round. SL ST at the end of the round to complete final work. Fasten off. Weave in ends.

## APPLYING THE APPLIQUE

Using fabric glue adhesive or hot glue gun, apply glue to the back of the applique and set it upon the middle of the FRONT of the TOP, securing it in place.

# THE CLUELESS
# CROCHET SKIRT

Unleash your inner Cher from *Clueless* in this mini skirt! She set the trend for the skirt suit look of the '90s, and the tradition lives on with this updated version. Her iconic fluffy cuffs have been moved to the hem of the skirt to add a splash of playfulness to the outfit. Warning: it might cause you to say "*Whatever!*" when you wear this.

## MATERIALS

YARN: Big Twist Value Worsted Yarn; 100% Acrylic (364 yards/347 meters); medium #4 Medium Rose (Color A): 2 skeins
Lion Brand Go For Faux Thick & Quick Yarn; 100% Acrylic (24 yards/22 meters); weight #7 Baked Alaska (Color B): 1 skein (project used less than half each skein)

HOOK: US size 7 (4.5mm) crochet hook and US size K/10.5 (6.5mm)

EXTRAS: craft scissors, measuring tape, safety pin, yarn needle, sewing needle, matching thread, Dritz ½ Braided Elastic 4-½ yards

GAUGE: 11 DC STS/5 DC ROWS = 4" using the smaller hook

## MEASUREMENTS

15 inches length

## SIZING

XS: [28 inches width]

SM: [30 inches width]

M: [32 inches width]

L: [35 inches width]

XL: [39 inches width]

2XL: [43 inches width]

3XL: [47 inches width]

4XL: [50 inches width]

# THE PATTERN

The shirt begins with the waistband worked flat. Crochet a horizontal piece that will be sewn around the elastic band. Once complete, the skirt is worked in the round from the top down.

## STARTING THE WAISTBAND

Crochet to the Sizing Amount:

XS: CH 96 [28 inches width]

S: CH 104 [30 inches width]

M: CH 112 [32 inches width]

LG: CH 123 [35 inches width]

XL: CH 137 [39 inches width]

2XL: CH 151 [43 inches width]

3XL: CH 166 [47 inches width]

4XL: CH 177 [50 inches width]

**R1:** CH 1, SC into all of the 96 (104, 112, 123, 137, 151, 166, 177) STS the entire row, turn work when complete.

**R2:** CH 2, HDC into all of the STS the entire row, turn work when complete.

**R3-R6:** Repeat R1-R2, alternating method (R3 = SC, R4 = HDC), until you reach row 6. Once you reach R6, SL ST to complete work. Fasten off. Weave in ends.

## ELASTIC BAND MEASUREMENTS

Cut a half inch more of the elastic so that the band overlaps when sewn together.

XS: [28.5 inches width]

S: [30.5 inches width]

M: [32.5 inches width]

LG: [35.5 inches width]

XL: [39.5 inches width]

2XL: [43.5 inches width]

3XL: [47.5 inches width]

4XL: [50.5 inches width]

Fold the horizontal crochet piece entirely in half. Thread the yarn to sew the folded crochet piece together.

Leave the sides of the piece open, so that the elastic can go through. Cut the yarn. Weave in ends.

## CONNECTING THE ELASTIC BAND ● ● ● ● ● ● ● ● ● ● ● ● ● ● ● ● ● ● ● ●

With the safety pin attached to the elastic, guide the elastic through the crochet band. Scrunch to guide the elastic through the crocheted band. Once it is in accordingly, thread your sewing needle with matching thread, overlap the elastic ends for a snug fit and sew the elastic together.

**Note:** Make sure it is thread incredibly tightly for security! Cut thread and knot.

## CREATING THE BOTTOM OF THE SKIRT ● ● ● ● ● ● ● ● ● ● ● ● ● ● ● ● ●

Working from the BOTTOM ROW of the crocheted band to the actual finished bottom of the skirt. Working in rounds, connect with SL ST after every completed round to continue work. Insert your hook into the bottom ST of the band to start work. (Note: Where it was sewn together.)

Bottom Length: 13 inches

**RND1:** Rejoin yarn with SL ST, CH 2, HDC into all the STS [97 (105, 113, 123, 137, 151, 167, 177) STS] for the entire round. At the end of the round, SL ST to continue work.

**RND2:** CH 4, TRC in first ST, *TRC TWO TIMES, TRC; repeat from * until the end of the round, SL ST at end of the round to continue work.

**Note:** Extend rounds within this section for personal desired length.

**RND3-RND14:** CH 4, TRC into all the STS for all the rounds. At the end of each round, SL ST to continue work. SL ST at the end of the final round to complete final work. Fasten off. Weave in ends.

Switch yarn.

Using K/10 6.5mm hook.

**RND1:** [Color B] CH 2, HDC into all the STS for the entire round, SL ST at the end of the round to complete final work. Fasten off. Weave in ends.

# THE AS IF! FLORAL BEANIE

Feel light and free in this chic cap, inspired by the hat Dionne from *Clueless* wore! It's a close-fitting cap that's comfortable, yet makes a statement with its floral design all around the rim. Wear it with your more flowing outfits for an interesting contrast or floral garments for a flowery overload. Versatility is the name of the game, and this cap has that in spades.

## MATERIALS

YARN: Red Heart Super Saver; 100% Acrylic (364 yards/198 meters); medium #4 White (Color A), Pale Yellow (Color B): 1 skein each (project used less than half each skein)

HOOK: US size 7 (4.5mm) crochet hook

EXTRAS: craft scissors, measuring tape, fabric glue or hot glue gun, yarn needle

GAUGE: 5 DC ROWS = 4"

## MEASUREMENTS

7 inches length

# THE PATTERN

With Color B, CH 2, SL ST to connect the last ST to the very first ST, creating a mini circle.

**RND1:** CH 2 (counts as a HDC), into the middle of the circle, HDC 5 TIMES, to create your first round. At the end of the round, SL ST to connect and continue work. [6 STS TOTAL]

**RND2:** CH 2 (counts as a HDC) HDC into the same ST, *HDC TWO TIMES into the following ST; repeat from * until the end of the round. At the end of the round, SL ST to connect and continue work. [12 STS TOTAL]

**RND3:** CH 2 (counts as a HDC), HDC TWO TIMES into the next ST, *HDC into the following ST, HDC TWO TIMES into the next ST; repeat from * until the end of the round. At the end of the round, SL ST to connect and continue work. [18 STS TOTAL]

**RND4:** CH 2 (counts as a HDC), HDC into the following ST, HDC TWO TIMES into the next ST, HDC into the following two STS; repeat from * until the end of the round. At the end of the round, SL ST to connect and continue work. [24 STS TOTAL]

**RND5:** CH 3 (counts as a DC) *SK 2 STS, in the next ST, (DC, CH 1, DC) all into the same ST; repeat from * until 2 STS remain at the end of the round, SK 1, DC in last ST, SL ST to connect and continue work.

**RND6:** CH 3 (counts as a DC), SK 1 ST, *into the CH 1 space, (2 DC, CH 1, 2 DC) all into the same space; repeat from * until the end of the round, ending on DC in last ST, SL ST to connect and continue work.

**RND7:** CH 3 (counts as a DC), SK 2 STS, *into the CH 1 space, (2 DC, CH 1, 2 DC) all into the same space, CH 1; repeat from * until the end of the round, ending on DC in last ST, SL ST to connect and continue work.

**RND8:** CH 3 (counts as a DC), *SK 2 STS, into the CH 1 space, (2 DC, CH 1, 2 DC) all into the same space, CH 1, DC in next CH 1 space, DC in next CH 1 space; repeat from * until the end of the round, ending on a DC ST in the last ST, SL ST to connect and continue work.

**RND9:** CH 3 (counts as a single DC) *SK 2 STS, *(3 DC, CH 1, 3 DC) in CH 1 space, SK 2, CH 1, DC in DC, CH 1; repeat from * ending with a DC in the last DC ST.

**RND10-RND13:** CH 3 (counts as a DC) *SK 3, *(3 DC, CH 1, 3 DC) in CH 1, SK 3, CH 1, DC in next DC, CH 1; repeat from * ending on the last DC ST, SL ST to join. Fasten off. Weave in ends.

## CREATING THE FLOWERS

### Crochet Flowers (Make 8 Total)

Using Color B, CH 2, SL ST to connect the last ST to the very first ST, creating a mini circle.

**RND1:** CH 2 (counts as a HDC), into the middle of the circle, HDC 5 TIMES, to create your first round. At the end of the round, SL ST to complete work. [6 STS TOTAL]

Fasten off. Weave in ends.

## CREATING THE PETALS

Using Color A, reinsert hook to the starting CHAIN.

**RND1:** CH 4 (counts as a TRC), then work (DC, HDC, SL ST) all into the same ST, CH 3, *(TRC, DC, HDC, SL ST) all into the next ST, then into the same ST, CH 3; repeat from * until the end of the round, SL ST to complete work. Fasten off. Weave in ends.

## APPLYING THE FLOWERS

Using fabric glue adhesive or a hot glue gun, add the glue to the center back of the flowers appliques and secure them to the final round at the bottom of the hat onto the 3 DC.

Sew the flowers on the final round bottom of the hat. With a strand of yarn, thread your yarn needle. Place the base of the flower onto the bottom round. Guide the needle through the hat and the flower base, weaving and securing the flower onto the hat. Knot and cut. Weave in the ends for each flower.

# THE CHARMED LIFE
# CROCHET BAG

You can never have enough accessories, especially when you can happily create and customize them to fit your own personal style! This super fluffy, phat crochet bag is an absolute must to accessorize any outfit.

NOTE: Be sure to experiment with different charms and accessories for your bag!

## MATERIALS

YARN: Bernat Baby Blanket; 100% Polyester (72 yards/65 meters); super bulky #6 Baby Teal: 2 skeins

HOOK: US size L (8mm) crochet hook

EXTRAS: (20) 10MM metal jump rings, (20) assorted charms, craft scissors, measuring tape, pliers (to open the jump rings), 2 [9 × 12] felt squares or 2 fabric fat squares (baby blue), fabric glue or hot glue gun, needle, matching thread, fabric pen, yarn needle.

GAUGE: 7 HDC STS/4 HDC ROWS= 4"

## MEASUREMENTS

8.5 inches length × 13 inches width

# THE PATTERN

## CREATING THE FRONT AND BACK PANEL OF THE BAG ·····················

This step is to construct two panels for the FRONT and BACK of the bag.

### Front

CH FOR 21 STS.

**R1-R10:** CH 2, HDC across into all the STS for all of the rows. At end of each row, turn work to continue. At final row, SL ST to complete work for this section. Fasten off. Weave in ends

### Back

CH FOR 21.

**R1-R10:** CH 2, HDC across into all the STS for all the rows. At end of each row, turn work to continue. At final row, SL ST to complete work for this section. Fasten off. Weave in ends

## SEWING THE BACK AND FRONT PANELS TOGETHER ·····················

Next, utilizing your yarn sewing needle and 3 sets of a long strand of yarn, sew both vertical sides and the bottom horizontal of the bag, FRONT AND BACK together, leaving the top open.

## ATTACHING THE FABRIC LINING

Turn back inside out. Cut 2 SETS of fabric from the fat square or felt square to the circumference of the finished crochet FRONT AND BACK PANEL pieces a little less than [8.5 inches length × 13 inches width]. Either sew or utilize fabric glue adhesive to apply to the back of the finished crochet pieces to secure it in place.

## CREATING THE PURSE STRAP

Creating one row to construct the strap for the bag.

Rejoin hook into the side corner of the BAG with a SL ST.

CH for 25 STS (17 inches length).

SL ST to connect to the other side of the bag.

Then, CH 2 and HDC into the same ST, and HDC back into all the 25 STS for the row. Once you reach the beginning ST, then SL ST to complete work for this section. Fasten off. Weave in ends.

## IMPLEMENTING THE CHARMS

Adding your charms to the metal jump rings, open the clasp to insert the jump ring into the Front Panel of the bag, into and between the STS, wherever you choose!

# THE CLUELESS PEN

Use the leftover yarn from the Clueless Crochet Skirt project to create the perfect accessory to match your handmade skirt!

## MATERIALS

YARN: Big Twist Value Worsted Yarn; 100% Acrylic (364 yards/347 meters); medium #4 Medium Rose (Color A), (used leftover yarn from project)
Lion Brand Go For Faux Thick & Quick Yarn; 100% Acrylic (24 yards/22 meters); weight #7 Baked Alaska (Color B), 1 skein (project used less than half each skein)

EXTRAS: scissors, hot glue gun or fabric adhesive, writing utensil (pen or pencil)

# INSTRUCTIONS

With leftover Color A, apply glue to the top of the pen or pencil.

Attach the yarn by wrapping around the pen or pencil, glue as you proceed around and down the writing utensil.

Once complete, apply glue to the top of the writing utensil, bunching, scrunching Color B around the top, securing in place.

# EXTRA INSPIRATION

Here are some other designs created to inspire you to explore other colors, patterns, and fashions throughout the decades!

RETRO CROCHET

RETRO CROCHET

RETRO CROCHET

RETRO CROCHET

# RESOURCES

These are some of my favorite places to find yarn and supplies!

- ❖ JOANN FABRIC AND CRAFTS
  JOANN.COM

- ❖ MICHAELS
  MICHAELS.COM

- ❖ RED HEART SUPER SAVER YARN
  A division of SPINRITE
  www.yarnspirations.com/red-heart-super-saver

- ❖ AMAZON.COM

- ❖ THE DREAM CROCHET
  Visit thedreamcrochet.com for my patterns, tutorials, and more!

# ACKNOWLEDGEMENTS

There were so many creative dreams that I held so near to my heart growing up, and one day, having the opportunity to create a book was entirely one of them. Thank you to Kelly Reed for the opportunity and Tian Connaughton for polishing the edits. So truly grateful! I am appreciative for the moment to set these creations into reality and onto pages that will always cast an eternal light within me. So, I am beyond thankful for everyone one who supported, hoped, and celebrated, or even smiled at my designs.

This book was formed with the truest hope to inspire. To exhibit the opportunity to construct and create what you would love to see. That is how I discovered the world of crochet, desiring to make whatever inspired me. Self-expression is such a vital aspect of life and having a stream of creativity is entirely a quality I am beyond grateful for.

Thank you to my parents, Mimi and Ed, for always pushing me to go for my aspirations, to create, maintain sheer ambition, to hope, and for supporting me every single step of the way. To have parents such as you two is truly beyond a gift in itself. Love you both tremendously!

Thank you to my brothers, Chris and Ethan, for your prodigious talents will always continue to inspire me. I am elated to have such a constant (and the best) sibling team by my side, as I am by yours always, creating art and ideas and eternally helping each other reach for the stars. You guys are the best!

It was a Family Craft Night in Delaware where I was first introduced to the art of crochet, and the love for it grew stitch by stitch. Incredibly indebted for that cherished memory and for a family that crafts! Thank you to my family and friends, who continue to encourage and support me. The positive energy you have constantly shown is insurmountable and I will always be grateful.

Wholeheartedly, I want to thank everyone who has shown crafty love and supported The Dream Crochet. Your appreciation is a fuel that sparks such creativity and elation within me, and I am truly overwhelmed with the opportunity to share these ideas with you all. You inspire me a great deal, and for you, I am eternally grateful and truly full of true creative bliss.

# ABOUT THE AUTHOR

Ashlee Elle is a crochet designer and creator, model, and photographer. Her work has been featured in numerous publications including *Simply Crochet*, *WeCrochet*, and *Crochet Now*. She earned a bachelor's degree in broadcast journalism and utilized her artistic education to create a small handmade business online. Her unique and original crochet patterns can be found on www.thedreamcrochet.com and in her Etsy shop: The Dream Crochet Shoppe. Connect with Ashlee Elle on Instagram @thedreamcrochet. Be sure to tag your handmade and WIP creations with #DreamItYourself!

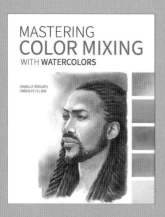
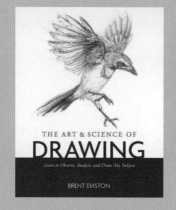
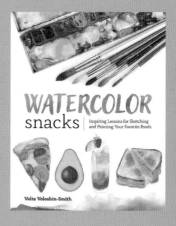
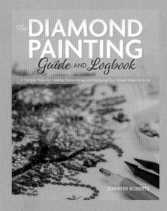
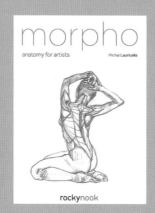
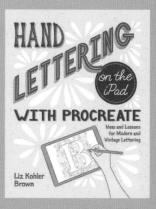